CW01086429

LONDON STORIES

OLD AND NEW

A lucky dip into London's traditions,
curiosities and anecdotal history.

First published a century ago

Written and edited
by
John O'London

Old House Books
Moretonhampstead, Devon
www.OldHouseBooks.co.uk

Old House Books produce facsimile copies of long out of print books that we believe deserve a second innings. Our reprints of detailed Victorian and Edwardian maps and guide books are of interest to genealogists and local historians. Other titles have been chosen to explore the 'why' and 'how' of life in years gone by and are of interest to anyone who wishes to know a bit more about the lives of our forebears.

For details of other Old House Books titles see the final pages of this book and, for the most up to date illustrated information, please visit our website (www.OldHouseBooks.co.uk) or request a catalogue.

We promise not to bombard you with junk mail and we will never sell your details to another business.

These London Stories first appeared as magazine articles before the First World War.

This edition was published in 2003 by
Old House Books,
The Old Police Station,
Pound Street,
Moretonhampstead,
Newton Abbot,
Devon TQ13 8PA UK

Tel: 01647 440707 Fax: 01647 440202

info@OldHouseBooks.co.uk

www.OldHouseBooks.co.uk

Printed and bound in India

ISBN 1 873590 27 X

LONDON IN LITTLE

It is frequently said that no one knows less about London than the Londoner, but it does not seem to occur to his critics that the Londoner has to live in London and accept her stupendous calls on his energy and attention. He could endure no part of London if he were obsessed by the whole.

Thus the average Londoner will take knowledge of London only as he runs. But for it he is always eager, and you cannot meet him in club, essay society, or tavern without discovering that nothing interests him more than a London story, so it be human and neighbourly.

Many thousands of country visitors are interested not only in the " sights " of London, but in the endless romance which exhales from its everyday streets and hidden places.

Hence this little book. It is, frankly, a more or less lucky " dip " into London traditions, curiosities, and anecdotal history, making little pretence to form and none, of course, to comprehensiveness.

JOHN O' LONDON.

CONTENTS

LONDON STORIES

London: that great sea whose ebb and flow
At once is deaf and loud, and on the shore
Vomits its wrecks, and still howls on for more.
Yet in its depth what treasures!

Percy Bysshe Shelley.

HOW OLD IS LONDON?

Rome keeps every year the reputed birthday of Rome, and has recently celebrated the 2,679th. Londoners do not dream of keeping London's birthday, and yet grave historians have placed its origin as far back in antiquity as that of Rome itself. John Stow begins his Survey of London: " As the Roman writers, to glorify the city of Rome, derive the original thereof from gods and demi-gods, by the Trojan progeny, so Geoffrey of Monmouth, the Welsh historian, deduceth the foundation of this famous city of London, for the greater glory thereof, and emulation of Rome, from the same original." This tradition, however, is much older than Geoffrey of Monmouth.

☙

The story is that the great-grandson of Æneas of Troy, Brute, had come to Italy, but was exiled from it after accidentally shooting his father, Silucius, while chasing deer. He is said to have prayed the goddess Diana for help, and that, on her counsel, he went into France and there built the two cities which are now Tours and Turenne. Later, about the time that Eli was high priest of Israel, he arrived in Albion and, landing on our west coast, fought with and destroyed certain giants, and after that " possessed and enjoyed all this Realm and named it Briteyn after his own name." Richard Grafton, the early sixteenth-century chronicler, says that, having at last set eyes upon his kingdom, Brute resolved to build a city, and accordingly travelled through the land to find a convenient situation, and coming to the River Thames, he walked along the shore and at last pitched upon a place very fit for his purpose. Here, therefore, he built a city, which he called NEW TROY, or Troynovant, under which name it continued a long time afterwards.

☙

After Brute there reigned a long, dim, and

splendid line of kings in Troynovant, who have left to posterity no more than their unpronounceable names; and after them, that king of fame, Lud, who put a strong wall about the city of Troynovant, and in the wall " a strong and fair gate, which he called Lud-gate; and because he loved this city, and used much and often to lie therein, he called it Caer Lud." Lud, also we are told, for the love he bore his city, gave great feasts and public entertainments. He commanded the citizens to build houses and other structures, and himself built in London innumerable towers, " so that no foreign country to a great distance round could show more beautiful palaces." When King Lud died, he was buried in his own Ludgate. He was succeeded by his brother, Cassibelan, in the eighth year of whose reign Julius Cæsar landed in Britain and the curtain of London's authentic history began to rise.

But, you may say, Surely all this is nonsensical fable!

It is.

DR. JOHNSON AND THE OLD CHESHIRE CHEESE.

Hundreds of people, including many Americans, resort annually to the Old Cheshire Cheese in Wine Office Court, Fleet Street, in order to view—and to occupy if possible—the reputed seat of Dr. Johnson. And certainly the rough tables, the sawdust on the floor, and all the other quaintnesses of this unique old eating-place favour the idea that in " Johnson's seat " Johnson really sat. What, however, is the evidence? The tavern is not mentioned in Boswell's " Life," nor by any of the Doctor's contemporaries who wrote their impressions of the great man. But this proves nothing. There are a great many days in Johnson's Fleet Street life of which we have no record. He lived close to the Cheese, and he was a frequenter of taverns. It seems unlikely that he was never in it. Tradition says he went to the Cheshire Cheese, and two writers, an Englishman and an American, have stated that they met men who saw him there. These are Cyrus Redding and Cyrus Jay. All the evidence comes from the two Cyruses.

♣

Cyrus Jay's book, " The Law: What I have Seen, What I have Heard, and What I have Known," was published in 1867. In it he writes: " I may here mention that when I first visited the house I used to meet several very old gentlemen who remembered Dr. Johnson nightly at the Cheshire Cheese, and they have told me, what is not generally known, that the Doctor, whilst living in the Temple, always went to the Mitre or the Essex Head; but when he removed to Gough Square and Bolt Court he was a constant visitor to the Cheshire Cheese, because nothing but a hurricane would have induced him to cross Fleet Street." It is curious that Jay should write (in 1867) that Johnson's connection with the Cheshire Cheese " is not generally known," because nine years earlier a like testimony had been published in Cyrus Redding's "Fifty Years' Recollections." Redding wrote explicitly:—

I often dined at the Mitre and the Cheshire Cheese. Johnson and his friends, I was informed, used to do the same, and I was told I should see individuals who had met them there ; this I found to be correct. The company was more select than in later times. Johnson had been dead above twenty years, but there were Fleet Street tradesmen who well remembered both Johnson and Goldsmith in those places of entertainment. There was a Mr. Tyers, a silk-merchant on Ludgate Hill, and Colonel Lawrence, who carried the colours of the Twentieth Regiment at the battle of Minden, ever fond of repeating that his regimental comrades bore the brunt on that celebrated day. The evening was the time we thus met. . . .

The left-hand room, entering the " Cheshire," and the table on the right upon entering that room, having the window at the end, was the table occupied by Johnson and his friends almost uniformly. This table and the room are now as they were when I first saw them, having had the curiosity to visit them recently. They were, and are still, as Johnson and his friends left them in their time. Johnson's seat was in the window, and Goldsmith sat on his left hand.

Except for the phrase "in the window," the bearing which seems doubtful, this agrees with the present claims of the Cheshire Cheese, and with the belief which occasionally transforms this resort of journalists into a parterre of pretty women escorted thither by a Cabinet Minister or an Ambassador.

♣　　♣　　♣

"HERE LIES NANCY DAWSON."

Nancy Dawson was a prodigious favourite with the town in the middle of the eighteenth century, and her name is still fragrant. Somewhere in the burial-ground of St. George the Martyr and St. George's, Bloomsbury, now a recreation ground, behind the Foundling Hospital, there was a stone bearing the simple inscription:—

HERE LIES NANCY DAWSON,

but this stone, which has been frequently inquired for, has long been missing. Some thirty years ago, when the burial-ground was laid out for recreation, careful search was made for interesting gravestones, and among those found was the tombstone of Zachary Macaulay, father of Lord Macaulay. But the resting-place of the blithe ballad singer who won the heart of London never came to light.

♣

Nancy Dawson was the daughter of a Clare Market porter, and was born about the year 1730. Clare Market is now swallowed up in Kingsway. She is said to have been brought up in poverty in a Drury Lane cellar, but at the age of sixteen she joined the company of a showman named Griffin, and appeared as a dancer at Sadler's Wells. Her dainty figure and personal style of dancing at once brought her into notice. She appeared again at Sadler's Wells as a Columbine, and soon afterwards had the glory of appearing at Covent Garden Theatre. Here in 1759 her great opportunity came. The man who danced the hornpipe in Gay's " Beggar's Opera " fell ill, and Nancy took his place. At once the playgoers took her to their hearts; she was " vastly celebrated, admired, imitated, and followed by everybody." When children sing " Here we go round the Mulberry Bush " they do so to the tune of Nancy Dawson's hornpipe in the "Beggar's Opera," as played at Covent Garden in 1759. A delightful tribute to Nancy is the song called "Ballad of Nancy Dawson," written at the time by George Alexander Stevens to be sung to the same air. The words are as follows:—

> Of all the girls in our town,
> The black, the fair, the red, the brown,
> That dance and prance it up and down,
>   There's none like Nancy Dawson.
>
> Her easy mien, her shape so neat,
> She foots, she trips, she looks so sweet,
> Her ev'ry motion's so complete,
>   I'd die for Nancy Dawson.

There is a good deal more of it. Nancy Dawson's portrait is one of the treasures of the Garrick Club to-day.

♣   ♣   ♣

THE KING OF BOOTMAKERS.

Hoby, of St. James's Street, was not only the greatest and most fashionable bootmaker of the Regency period; incidentally, he was a Methodist preacher at Islington. He employed some three hundred workmen, and was wont to say what he pleased to his customers, whom his humour sometimes annoyed. Horace Churchill, an ensign in the Guards, one day entered Hoby's shop in a great passion, saying that his boots were so ill-made that he should never employ Hoby for the future. Hoby gravely called to his shopman, " John, close the shutters. It is all over with us. I must shut up shop. Ensign Churchill withdraws his custom from me."

♣

While he was attending the Duke of Kent to try on some boots, the news arrived of Lord Wellington's victory over the French army at Vittoria. The Duke was kind enough to mention the glorious news to Hoby, who coolly said: " If Lord Wellington had had any other bootmaker than myself, he would never have had his great and constant success; for my boots and prayers bring his lordship out of all his difficulties." He was bootmaker to the Duke of Wellington from his boyhood, and received innumerable orders in the Duke's handwriting, both from the Peninsula and France, which he always preserved. On one occasion Sir John Shelley came into Hoby's shop to complain that his top-boots had split in several places. Hoby quietly said: " How did that happen,

Sir John?" "Why, in walking to my stables."
"Walking to your stables?" said Hoby, with
a sneer; "I made the boots for riding, not
walking."

♣

Hoby was bootmaker to George III, the
Prince of Wales, the royal Dukes, and many
officers in the Army and Navy. His shop was
at the top of St. James's Street, at the corner
of Piccadilly, next to the old Guards' Club. He
was the first man who drove about London in
a tilbury. It was painted black, and drawn by
a beautiful black cob. He died worth a hundred
and twenty thousand pounds.

♣ ♣ ♣

A PARISIAN ANSWERED.

A seventeenth-century Londoner, visiting
Paris, met a Parisian who, pointing proudly to
the Seine, asked, "Have you anything in London to compare with *that?*" The Londoner
replied, "Yes, and we call it Fleet Ditch."

♣ ♣ ♣

THE ROYAL EXCHANGE MOTTO.

Various statements have been made regarding
the origin, and cause of placing, of the motto on

the pediment of the Royal Exchange, London,
—" The earth is the Lord's, and the fullness
thereof,"—the general impression being that it
was suggested by Prince Albert. Sir William
Tite, M.P., architect of the Exchange, thus explained the matter: " As the work (the building
of the Exchange) proceeded, his Royal Highness
took much interest in the modelling and carving
of the various groups, and condescended very
frequently to visit the studio of the sculptor in
Wilton Place.

♣

" The reader may recollect that the figure of
Commerce stands on an elevated block or pedestal in the centre of the group, and it became a
subject of earnest consideration with Mr. Westmacott and myself in what way the plainness
of this block could be relieved; for although in
the original model, on a small scale, this defect
did not strike the eye, yet in the execution it
was very apparent. Wreaths, fasces, festoons,
were all tried, but the effect was unsatisfactory;
in this state of affairs Mr. Westmacott submitted
the difficulty to his Royal Highness. After a
little delay, Prince Albert suggested that the
pedestal in question would be a very appropriate
situation for a religious inscription . . . and
he particularly wished that such inscription

should be in English, so as to be intelligible to all. This happy thought put an end to all difficulty; and as Dr. Milman, the learned Dean of St. Paul's, had kindly advised me in reference to the Latin inscriptions on the frieze and in the Merchants' Area, Mr. Westmacott consulted him on this subject also; and he suggested the words of the Psalmist, which were at once adopted."

♣   ♣   ♣

MUCH LIKE LONDON.

Hell is a city much like London—
A populous and a smoky city;
There, are all sorts of people undone,
And there is little or no fun done;
Small justice shown, and still less pity.

Percy Bysshe Shelley.

THE APPLE WOMAN WHO ANNEXED HYDE PARK.

Seventy-five years ago a small shanty called the " White Cottage " stood at the east end of the Serpentine lake in Hyde Park, and in it a famous apple woman, named Ann Hicks, sold apples and gingerbread. Originally she had made use of an old conduit which stood on this spot, the site of which is marked by an inscribed monument to-day. When the conduit disappeared she plied her business at an open stall with an awning. Ann Hicks was an alert woman, and a born letter-writer. She wrote to Lord Lincoln, then Commissioner of Works and Forests, asking to be allowed to provide herself with a lock-up in which she could safely leave her goods at night. This was permitted. When a little later she asked the Woods and Forests' kind permission to erect a small brick enclosure there was some demur; nevertheless, Ann got her brick enclosure. The " enclosure " turned out to be four walls, provided with windows and a door. A little later she petitioned to increase its height, and this was allowed up to five feet. Then she begged to be allowed to mend the roof, and again authority yielded; but somehow, in the mending process, a chimney " not seen before by gods or wondering men " made its appearance. The chimney communicated with a fireplace.

♣

Ann Hicks was now a householder in Hyde Park, with exemptions and privileges all her own. She wrote again, asking to be allowed to place a hurdle round the house to prevent boys peeping into her window. By this time the habit of reluctant assent had taken such hold of the official mind that no difficulty was raised. Having set up her hurdles, the pioneering apple woman began to move them outwards by small degrees until they enclosed a snug domain. How much farther the territorial expansion of the apple-stall would have proceeded is now one of the unanswerable conjectures of history. Her troubles began when the Great Exhibition was planned and, in consequence, the removal of obstructions in the Park was ordered.

♣

Hicks was given notice to quit. She at once defied the Woods and Forests to remove her, claiming vested interests in the ground, and supported her case by a pleasingly "tall" story that her grandfather had saved George II from a watery grave in the Serpentine, and had been rewarded with the right to keep a stall in the Park. Lord Seymour, the Chief Commissioner, fairly wilted under Ann Hicks's scorn. At last, doubtful of his position, he took the matter to the Duke of Wellington as Ranger, by whom the whole matter was placed for inquiry in the hands of a solicitor. The result was that the bottom fell out of Ann Hicks's case, and for her actual rights, if any, she received a small allowance. Still keeping up the struggle, she placarded the trees in Hyde Park with her wrongs. An agitation was set up, and it was only when Mr. Bernal Osborne brought the matter before Parliament, and the Government had replied exhaustively, that the Hyde Park apple woman retired into private life.

♣   ♣   ♣

A FAMOUS PLAYER AT DRAUGHTS.

When passing Hanway Street, close to the foot of the Tottenham Court Road, you may notice that the tavern at the corner bears the name of the Blue Posts. This house (now re-built) was once kept by a man named Joshua Sturges. He was the author of a well-known "Guide to the Game of Draughts," published in 1800, and dedicated by permission to the Prince of Wales. Sturges's epitaph bore curious testimony to his skill as a draughts-player and his qualities as a man. Here it is, as preserved in an old volume of *Notes and Queries* :—

Sacred to the memory of Mr. Joshua Sturges. Many years a Respectable Licensed Victualler in this Parish; who departed this Life the 12th of August, 1813. Aged 55 years. He was esteemed for the many excellent Qualities he possessed, and his desire to improve the Minds, as also to benefit the Trade of his Brother Victuallers.

25

His Genius was also eminently displayed to create innocent and rational amusement to Mankind, in the Production of his Treatise, on the difficult game of Draughts, which Treatise received the Approbation of his Prince, and many other Distinguished Characters. . . .

May his Virtues be rewarded in the next. Peace to his Soul, and respected be his Memory.

This epitaph was one of the many curiosities of Old St. Pancras churchyard, but it has long been obliterated.

♣ ♣ ♣

"THE RATCATCHER'S DAUGHTER."

Among old London songs which have attained to a certain classic rank there are few more racy of the London of the last mid-century than "The Ratcatcher's Daughter." It was introduced to London by Sam Cowell, then a famous singer. The lyric tells its own story, and it would be a pity not to give it complete:—

Not long ago in Vestminster
   There liv'd a ratcatcher's daughter,—
But she didn't quite live in Vestminster,
   'Cause she liv'd t'other side of the vater;—
Her father caught rats, and she sold sprats
   All round and about that quarter;
And the gentlefolks all took off their hats,
   To the putty little ratcatcher's daughter.

   Doodle dee! doodle dum! di dum doodle da!

She vore no 'at upon 'er 'ead,
  No cap nor dandy bonnet,—
The 'air of 'er 'ead all 'ung down her back,
  Like a bunch of carrots upon it ;—
Ven she cried " Sprats ! " in Vestminster,
  She 'ad such a sweet loud woice, sir,
You could hear her all down Parliament Street,
  As far as Charing Cross, sir.

    Doodle dee ! doodle dum ! di dum doodle da !

Now, rich and poor, both far and near,
  In matrimony sought her ;
But at friends and foes she turn'd up her nose,
  Did the putty little ratcatcher's daughter.
For there was a man cried " Lily-vite Sand,"
  In Cupid's net had caught her ;
And right over head and ears in love
  Vent the putty little ratcatcher's daughter.

    Doodle dee, etc.

Now Lily-vite Sand so ran in her 'ead,
  As she vent along the Strand, oh,
She forgot as she'd got sprats on her 'ead,
  And cried, " D'ye vant any lily-vite sand, oh,"
The folks, amaz'd, all thought her craz'd,
  As she vent along the Strand, oh.
To see a girl vith sprats on her 'ead
  Cry, " D'ye vant any lily-vite sand, oh."

    Doodle dee, etc.

Now Ratcatcher's Daughter so ran in *his* 'ead,
  He couldn't tell vat he was arter,
So, instead of crying " D'ye vant any sand ? "

27

He cried, " D'ye vant any ratcatcher's darter ? "
His donkey cock'd his ears and laughed,
   And couldn't think vat he was arter,
Ven he heard his lily-vite sandman cry,
     " D'ye vant any ratcatcher's daughter ? "
     Doodle dee, etc.

They both agreed to married be
   Upon next Easter Sunday,
But Ratcatcher's Daughter she had a dream
   That she wouldn't be alive on Monday ;
She vent vunce more to buy some sprats,
   And she tumbled into the vater,
And down to the bottom, all kiver'd with mud,
   Vent the putty little Ratcatcher's Daughter.
     Doodle dee, etc.

Ven Lily-vite Sand 'e 'eard the news,
   His eyes ran down with vater,
Said 'e, " In love I'll constiant prove ;
   And blow me if I'll live long arter."
So he cut 'is throat vith a pane of glass
   And stabb'd 'is donkey arter !
So 'ere is an end of Lily-vite Sand,
   Donkey, and the Ratcatcher's Daughter.
     Doodle dee, etc.

The neighbours all, both great and small,
   They flocked unto 'er berrein',
And vept that a gal who'd cried out sprats,
   Should be dead as any herrein'.
The Corioner's Inquest on her sot,
   At the sign of the Jack i' the Vater

To find what made life's sand run out
  Of the putty little Ratcatcher's Daughter.
    Doodle dee, etc.

The werdict was that too much vet
  This poor young voman died on ;
For she made an ole in the Riviere Thames,
  Vot the penny steamers ride on.
'Twas a haccident they all agreed,
  And nuffink like self-slaughter ;
So not guiltee o' fell in the sea,
  They brought in the Ratcatcher's Daughter.

Well, ladies and gentlemen—arter the two bodies were resusticated—they buried them both in one seminary ; and the epigram which they writ upon the tombstone went as follows :—Doodle dee, etc.,

    Doodle dee, etc.

The song has the tang of its period.

♣   ♣   ♣

THREE POETS IN ONE COURT SUIT.

Shortly after he had accepted the Poet Laureateship (offered him at the age of seventy-four by Sir Robert Peel), William Wordsworth came to London, being invited to attend a State Ball in his new character. Grasmere's lake was exchanged for London streets. " And will you put on a Court dress? " said Haydon, the painter. To " Daddy " Wordsworth this was an unforeseen problem. He had no Court dress, and probably had little liking for the expense of obtaining one. Who should come to the rescue but Samuel Rogers? Rogers was always coming to the rescue. He fitted up Wordsworth with a shabby Court suit of his own. True, Wordsworth was twice Rogers's size, and was only got into the clothes by much pulling and hauling. Thus attired, and with Sir Humphry Davy's sword whipping his shins, the venerable poet presented himself before his Queen.

♣

But the awkwardness of Poet Laureates is not easily exhausted. Five years later Wordsworth died, and on November 5th, 1850, Tennyson received a letter offering him the Laureateship in succession to Wordsworth. To him, in turn, came an invitation to Court, and with it the same problem of a suitable dress. Rogers's greatness of mind asserted itself again. He had himself been offered the Laureateship, but had refused it on the score of old age. He had seen one poet forced into his shabby old Court suit. Why not another? Hearing of Tennyson's difficulty, he promptly offered him those versatile garments. And Tennyson wore them;

the coat did well enough, but his friends were consumed with anxiety about the nether garments, which he did not try on until the fateful morning.

♣ ♣ ♣

A WOMAN'S NAME ON A WALL.

Little more than thirty years ago some masons, who were doing some odd jobs in the Tower of London, found behind a wooden mantelpiece a faint signature on the wall which was believed to be that of Margaret Roper, the beloved married daughter of Sir Thomas More. One or two of the letters were obliterated, but the position of the R's strongly supported the assumption. The wrench of a crowbar had recalled a great tragedy. For the story behind that signature was that of Sir Thomas More's confinement in the Tower and his death for conscience's sake. It was the story of his beautiful home life at Chelsea, with its art, its music, its wit, and its boundless hospitality. It was the story of that living interment in the Tower which he declared was the realisation of his youthful dreams of a monastic life. But for his wife and children, he said, he would long ago have closed himself in " as strait a room, and straiter, too." Nor was this idle talk; for,

c 2

even in his cell, Sir Thomas was discovered by one of his daughters wearing a hair shirt. Portions of that vestment are still in existence.

♣

But his wife and children were not content to regard his imprisonment as a spiritual exercise. Tragic, humorous and life-like is William Roper's account of Lady More's visit to her husband in his cell. She was a good, respectable soul, who loved her home, her regular ways, her larder keys, and of course her husband. But she did not love that irregularity in him which made him stand out against admitting the ecclesiastical " supremacy " of Henry VIII. When, therefore, this correct lady picked her way into her lord's cell, much afraid of locks and bolts and suffocation, " Mr. More," she said, " I marvel that you, that hitherto have been taken for a wise man, will now so play the fool. And seeing you have at Chelsea a right fair house, your library, gallery, garden, orchard, and all other necessaries so handsome about you, where you might in the company of me, your children, and household be merry, I muse what in God's name you mean thus fondly to tarry." To which More, strong in his purpose, replied, " Is not this house as nigh heaven as mine own ? " Lady More's answer was short, woman-like, inevitable. " *Twittle twattle, twittle twattle!* " she said, rustling her gown of many folds.

♣

Very different were More's earnest talks with his beloved daughter, Margaret Roper, though she, too, tried to change her father's views. Finding her examples and instances useless, she exclaimed, in sad and humorous despair, " I see not what to say more unless I should look to persuade you with the reason that Master Harry Pattensen made." Pattensen had been Sir Thomas's fool, and was now in the service of the Lord Mayor. Said Meg: " He met one day one of our men, and when he had asked where you were, and heard that you were in the Tower still, he waxed angry with you, and said, ' Why? What aileth him that he will not swear? Wherefore should he stick to swear? I have sworn the oath myself.' And so," says Margaret, " have I sworn." At this More laughed, and said, " That word was like Eve, for she offered Adam no worse fruit than she had eaten herself."

♣

Who can tell how or when Margaret Roper

scratched her name over that forgotten mantelpiece? Perhaps she did it wearily, while her father maintained by argument his fatal resolution. Perhaps it was done to fill a few minutes of suspense. Perhaps she desired to link her name at least to the spot where he who had tended her mind like a garden was to take leave of life. In vain mother and daughters petitioned the King through Richard Cromwell. The story moves swiftly to its end. For very shame the King commuted the sentence of drawing, hanging and quartering at Tyburn into beheading on Tower Hill. It was Sir Thomas Pope, an old friend of More's, who brought the King's message that he must die on the 6th of July, before nine o'clock. " The King's pleasure is farther," said Pope, " that at your execution you shall not use many words." When More's head had been exposed on London Bridge for a month, it was Margaret Roper who bribed the man whose business it was to throw it into the river to give it to her. Well does this exquisite lady take her place in Tennyson's " Dream of Fair Women," between Rosamond and Joan of Arc. Looking at Holbein's portrait of the More family, the great Erasmus, who had been their guest, wrote to Margaret: " I recognise you all, but no one better than yourself. I seem to behold through all your beautiful household a soul shining forth still more beautiful."

♣   ♣   ♣

THE ONLY MEETING OF NELSON AND WELLINGTON.

The following conversation took place at Walmer Castle on October 1st, 1834. "We were talking (says John Wilson Croker) of Lord Nelson, and some instances were mentioned of the egotism and vanity that derogated from his character. 'Why,' said the Duke, 'I am not surprised at such instances, for Lord Nelson was, in different circumstances, two quite different men, as I myself can vouch, though I only saw him once in my life, and for, perhaps, an hour. It was soon after I returned from India. I went to the Colonial Office in Downing Street, and there I was shown into the little waiting-room on the right hand, where I found, also waiting to see the Secretary of State, a gentleman, whom, from his likeness to his pictures and the loss of an arm, I immediately recognised as Lord Nelson.

♣

" He could not know who I was, but he entered at once into conversation with me, if I

35

can call it conversation, for it was almost all on his side, and all about himself, and in really a style so vain and so silly as to surprise and almost disgust me. I suppose something that I happened to say may have made him guess that I was somebody, and he went out of the room for a moment, I have no doubt to ask the office-keeper who I was, for when he came back he was altogether a different man, both in manner and matter.

&

"All that I had thought a charlatan style had vanished, and he talked of the state of this country and of the aspect and probabilities of affairs on the Continent with a good sense, and a knowledge of subjects both at home and abroad that surprised me equally and more agreeably than the first part of our interview had done; in fact, he talked like an officer and a statesman.

"The Secretary of State kept us long waiting, and certainly for the last half or three-quarters of an hour I don't know that I ever had a conversation that interested me more. Now, if the Secretary of State had been punctual, and admitted Lord Nelson in the first quarter of an hour, I should have had the same impression of a light and trivial character that other people have had, but luckily I saw enough to be satisfied that he was really a very superior man; but certainly a more sudden and complete metamorphosis I never saw."

This remarkable interview is the subject of a well-known engraving.

♣   ♣   ♣

LONDON AS A HIDING-PLACE.

It is not an easy thing to hide oneself in London. Scotland Yard sees to that, but even Scotland Yard can be baffled for quite a long time. Not many of us, bent on disappearance, could hope to emulate the ingenuity of Mr. Howe, who vanished early in the eighteenth century. Concealment in London was then as many times more difficult as the metropolis was smaller. Mr. Howe, a man of means and respectability, lived in Jermyn Street, and the story of his disappearance is told by Dr. William King in his " Political and Literary Anecdotes of His Own Times," which he wrote as a pastime during an illness. His acquaintance with Mr. Howe of Jermyn Street began about the year 1706.

♣

One morning Mr. Howe, telling his wife casually that he had business in the neighbourhood of the Tower, cheerfully left his home.

37

A few hours later Mrs. Howe received a note from her husband saying that urgent business called him to Holland, and that he was taking ship immediately, and might be absent two or three months. She did not see him again for seventeen years!

&

Then, one evening, while she was supping with some relatives and friends, a note was handed to her. On reading it she smiled, and handed it gaily to Dr. Rose, her brother-in-law, saying: " You see, brother, old as I am, I have got a gallant." The note requested her to meet the writer on the following evening in Birdcage Walk. On looking at it attentively, Dr. Rose exclaimed that the handwriting was no other than that of her long-vanished husband. Everyone was in consternation, and the widow, as she deemed herself, very properly fainted. Next evening, however, accompanied by Dr. Rose and other friends, she kept the appointment. They did not wait long before Mr. Howe quietly walked up to them and embraced his wife. The two went home together and lived in perfect harmony.

&

Then Mr. Howe's story came out. He had not been near the Tower, he had not been to

Holland. He had put on a black wig (he was a fair man) and had gone to live in a quiet street in Westminster. After his complete disappearance Mrs. Howe supposed that, unknown to herself, he had contracted some heavy debts; consequently for some weeks she went in fear of duns and bailiffs. However, nothing happened, and when all inquiries were exhausted Mrs. Howe reconciled herself to her loneliness. Before very long it became necessary for her to obtain a settlement of her husband's affairs, in order that she might have the means of living. She accordingly applied for a special Act of Parliament, and, extraordinary to relate, Mr. Howe, in his Westminster lodging, allowed the Bill to go through, and enjoyed reading of its progress in the gazettes at a little coffee-house.

⁂

Ten years passed, and during that period Mrs. Howe's two children died. Wishing to reduce her expenditure, she removed from her house in Jermyn Street to a smaller one in Brewer Street, in Soho, her movements being followed with watchful interest by her husband, who began more and more to appreciate the luxury of examining his wife, as it were, through a telescope. Opposite to the house in Brewer Street, a decent corn chandler, named

Salt, had his shop. Mr. Howe scraped acquaintance with Mr. Salt, and became so intimate with him as to dine at his house two or three times a week. On these occasions it was his pleasure to stand at the window and look across the way into his wife's drawing-room, where he watched her little comings and goings: Mr. Howe doubtless had his own reasons for his behaviour, but they never appeared, and it is not improbable that his escapade was a laborious whim.

♣ ♣ ♣

THE MARBLE ARCH.

The Marble Arch in Oxford Street, facing the site of " Tyburn Tree," was copied by its architect, John Nash, with much modification, from the Arch of Constantine at Rome, and its original position was in front of the chief entrance to Buckingham Palace. The archway, as first designed, was found to be too small to admit the Royal coach, but the mistake was remedied in time. A colossal bronze group emblematic of Victory was to have been the crowning ornament, but the intention was altered in favour of an equestrian statue of George IV, executed by Chantrey at a cost of 9,000 guineas. But this statue never reached the Marble Arch, and it is now in Trafalgar Square. In removing the Marble Arch to the Cumberland Gate (formerly the " Tyburn Gate ") of Hyde Park, an important and beautiful frieze was irreparably damaged, and has not been replaced. The sculptured decorations are by Flaxman, Westmacott, and Rossi, all men of talent. The big central gates are said to be the largest in Europe, and among the finest. The entire cost of the Arch was about £80,000. Paris paid £416,666 for her Arc de Triomphe. Some years ago the railings of Hyde Park were set back at this point in a wide crescent, but the Arch is left where it stood, with the result that it is now isolated in the roadway with traffic passing on both sides but never through it.

♣　　　♣　　　♣

THE WORLD WEIGHED AT CLAPHAM.

Henry Cavendish, " the modern Newton," and " the man who weighed the world," was born in 1731, four years after Newton's death. He was educated at a private school at Hackney, from which he passed to Peterhouse, Cambridge, which he left three years later, without a degree. Thereafter he was a man of science, devoting his whole life to experimental philosophy. "The man who weighed the world," wrote Henry Cavendish's cousin, great-grandfather of the present Duke of Devonshire, "buried his science and his wealth in solitude at Clapham." His science, however, he did not bury, for he published to the world certain facts which placed him in the first rank of experimental philosophers. It was he who converted oxygen and hydrogen into water, proving that water consists of these gases; it was he who first stated the difference between animal and common electricity; and it was he who, by a course of ingenious experiments, indicated the weight of the world—now prettily estimated at 6,000,000,000,000,000,000,000,000 tons.

♣

Cavendish had no vanity; he cared for no one's praise and avoided society. For money he cared little; up to his fortieth year he was comparatively poor, probably having an annual income of no more than £500; but in 1773 an uncle died, who left him an enormous fortune. Of that he spent very little, he was one of those rare men who have no idea of the uses of money. His personal needs were simple, and the fact that he was rich never seems to have struck him as a matter of importance. He was also a shy man, to whom it was difficult even to speak. Dr. Wollaston said: " The way to talk to Cavendish is never to look at him, but to talk, as it were, into vacancy, and then it is not unlikely you may set him going." He had few visitors, but his library was at the service of anyone who cared to use it. Yet, so anxious was he to be undisturbed, that he hired another house in which to accommodate his books, and paid a librarian to look after them. When he wanted to refer to his books he went round as though to a circulating library, and left a receipt for whatever he took away. His house at Clapham was practically a workshop; the upper rooms were converted into an observatory, the drawing-room—Cavendish had no use for a drawing-room—was a laboratory, and in an ante-room he had fixed up a forge. On the lawn he erected a stage which enabled him to reach the top of a large tree, on which secure and isolated perch he could be alone with his thoughts.

♣

As a host this strange being was hardly a success; the few people who were admitted to his table were always given the same fare— a leg of mutton. On one occasion four scientific men were to dine with him. When his housekeeper consulted him as to what she was to give them to eat, he said a leg of mutton. " Sir," said the good soul, " that will not be enough for five." " Well, then, get two," he replied. And this man who was content to eat mutton everlastingly had no sense of beauty; he cared for nothing beyond his own work. Women he hated; his usual method of communication with his housekeeper was by means of notes left on the hall table, and if any female servant came into his presence she was instantly dismissed. To guard against chance meetings with his household, he had a second staircase erected in his Clapham villa. Lord Brougham remembered " the shrill cry he uttered as he shuffled quickly from room to room, seeming to be annoyed if looked at, but sometimes approaching to hear what was passing among others."

♣

This extraordinary man left a fortune of £1,750,000; his heir, Lord George Cavendish, was permitted to see him only once a year, and then for no longer than half an hour. He never changed the fashion of his dress—a fact which naturally drew that attention to him which he was anxious to avoid. He was, indeed, a man of pure science in whose constitution there seemed little room for human feeling. He died on March 10th, 1810, aged seventy-eight and was buried in All Saints' Church, Derby. His great fortune went to Lord George Cavendish.

♣   ♣   ♣

LONDON'S QUEEREST STREET-NAME.

The most curious of London street-names is Crooked Usage in Chelsea. It probably dates from Saxon times when the land was divided into allotments, separated by breadths of unturned grass. These strips or " usages " were usually straight, but there was one crooked one, and the Crooked Usage, like the Ugly Duckling, has been favoured; it has survived as the name of a twentieth-century London street !

♣   ♣   ♣

THE ATHENÆUM CLUB.

The Athenæum Club in Pall Mall celebrated its one hundredth birthday only two years ago. Among those present at the preliminary meeting held on February 17th, 1824, were Sir Humphry Davy, the great chemist, John Wilson Croker, the biographer of Dr. Johnson, Sir Thomas Lawrence, the painter, Thomas Moore, and Sir Walter Scott. But it is doubtful whether Scott ever used the club. The classic building stands on a part of the old courtyard of Carlton House, the home of the Prince Regent, and is one of the most beautiful of its kind in London. Its most noticeable features are its frieze, copied from the great frieze of the Parthenon, and the figure of Minerva by Edward Hodges Baily, R.A., over the portico. The frieze was suggested by John Wilson Croker, if we may accept the epigram written at the time.

> I'm John Wilson Croker !
> I do what I please !
> They ask for an ice-house :
> I'll give them a frieze.

In its early days the club had some of its later reputation for silence and frigidity. Theodore Hook, the wit and practical joker, reigned supreme in his own corner, and it is said that when he disappeared from it the number of diners fell off by more than three hundred per annum. The corner was known as Temperance Corner, because to avoid hurting the susceptibilities of grave and dignified persons such as bishops, the orders for spirits were given to the waiters in terms of " toast-and-water " and " lemonade."

♣

Thackeray's first repulse, when he applied for membership, is an old story. His name was proposed by Dean Milman, who never doubted of success and was greatly distressed when his friend was rejected. Thackeray took his rebuff calmly. " I was quite prepared," he wrote to Abraham Hayward, " for the issue of the kind of effort made at the Athenæum on my behalf; indeed, as a satirical writer, I rather wonder that I have not made more enemies than I have." In 1851 his name was again brought forward, and he was elected. It was on the steps of the Athenæum Club that Thackeray and Dickens were reconciled after their estrangement. They met there by chance, and Thackeray, offering his hand, said that he could no longer bear to be on any but the old terms of friendship. A very few days later Dickens attended his old friend's funeral.

♣ ♣ ♣

THE GOLD-HEADED CANE.

A remarkable relic is preserved in the club-room of the Royal College of Physicians in Trafalgar Square. It is a gold-headed cane. The physician's gold-headed cane was once the symbol of his profession as definitely as the striped pole is the symbol still of the barber's.

The cane now so religiously preserved by the Royal College of Physicians was used, or

47

worn, by five successive members of the medical profession, each of whom left a great name; no single object is regarded by British physicians with more veneration. Oddly enough, it is not the typical physician's cane of bygone days. It is not, that is to say, a knobbed cane, whose knob was fitted with a lid opening into a vinaigrette or receptacle for disinfectants. It is a cross-handled cane, and the handle bears the engraved arms of each of its successive owners. Originally possessed by Dr. John Radcliffe, it was bequeathed by him to Dr. Richard Mead. But the dynasty is best put into form. This unique gold-headed cane descended as follows:

Dr. John Radcliffe (1650-1714).
|
Dr. Richard Mead (1673-1754).
|
Dr. Anthony Askew (1722-1774).
|
Dr. David Pitcairn (1749-1809).
|
Dr. Matthew Baillie (1761-1823).

When the Gold-headed Cane reached Dr. Baillie it had become a treasure too precious for ordinary use. Indeed, the custom of carrying a gold-headed cane had declined in the profession. Matthew Baillie, the renowned morbid anatomist, kept the sacred symbol in a corner of his consulting-room in Grosvenor Square, though he would occasionally take it with him when he was joining some circle of professional friends. He uttered precepts which might be used as annotations to Mr. Bernard Shaw's " Doctor's Dilemma." He would say: " I know better perhaps than any other man, from my knowledge of anatomy, how to discover a disease, but when I have done so I do not know better how to cure it." It was Baillie who told a fine lady with an imaginary ailment that she might eat oysters, shells and all. He died in 1823, and his bust is in Westminster Abbey.

♣   ♣   ♣

DON JUAN'S VISION OF LONDON.

A mighty mass of brick, and smoke, and ship-
      ping,
    Dirty and dusky, but as wide as eye
  Could reach, with here and there a sail just
      skipping
    In sight, then lost amidst the forestry
  Of masts; a wilderness of steeples peeping

49

On tip-toe through their sea-coal canopy;
A huge, dun cupola, like a foolscap crown
On a fool's head—and there is London town!

Byron.

♣   ♣   ♣

THE NELSON COLUMN.

Perhaps no letter to the *Times*, embodying a popular and practical proposal, has been more successful than the one which appeared in that newspaper on September 9th, 1837, signed "J. B." and expressed, in part, as follows:—

Allow me to suggest through your columns the favourable opportunity and most appropriate situation now afforded of erecting in the centre of the Square some worthy monument or statue, commemorating the glorious victories of the immortal Nelson.

The idea of honouring Nelson's memory in this manner was so favourably received that in the *Times* of April 27th, 1838, the following notice appeared: —

NELSON MONUMENT.—The committee for erecting a monument to the memory of Lord Nelson hereby give notice that they are desirous of receiving from architects, artists and other persons, designs for such a monument, to be erected in Trafalgar Square.

The committee cannot, in the present state of the subscriptions, fix definitely the sum to be expended, but they recommend that the estimated cost of the several designs should be confined within the sum of £20,000 to £30,000. This condition, and that of the intended site, are the only restrictions to which artists are limited.

Committees and meetings were organised, and the site as well as the monument was the subject of much debate. On February 22nd, 1838, a meeting was held at the Thatched House, in St. James's Street, at which it was resolved " that a subscription be raised for the purpose of creating a national monument in a conspicuous part of the metropolis." It is a somewhat forgotten, yet certainly an interesting, fact that the Trafalgar Square site was agreed upon at a meeting at the London Tavern presided over by the Duke of Wellington.

♣

The project moved slowly, and was destined to be an unconscionably long undertaking. In April, 1839, the *Gentleman's Magazine* was able to report the result of the competition:—

The first premium was adjudged by the Committee to the proposition of W. Railton, architect, for a fluted Corinthian column, 174 feet high, on a pedestal ornamented with reliefs, and surmounted by a statue 17 feet high. This design can, of course, make no pretension to originality ; and besides is open to various other objections.

But the second prize was awarded to Mr. E. H. Baily, R.A., and to him ultimately fell the commission for the statue. In 1840 the contract to erect the column within two years was given to Messrs. Ginsell and Peto, for the sum of £17,860. The foundation-stone of the great national monument was laid, strange to say, without ceremony. This was on September 30th, 1840. Despite the terms of the contract, it was three years before the raising of Baily's statue to the summit was begun. The figure, which stood 17 feet high and weighed 18 tons, was made of stone from the Duke of Buccleuch's Granton quarry. It was, of course, in segments, but these were put together on the ground so that the public might inspect the complete work. In the two days during which it was on view it was visited by 100,000 persons. The dimensions of the monument are :—

Steps (formerly between the Lions but now removed)	7
Pedestal	37
Column	105
Tambour	7
Statue	17
Total	173

Landseer's four lions were not placed in position

until 1867. They have been criticised and admired by different judges. Richard Jefferies plumply described them as " the only noble open-air work of native art in the four-million-city."

❧   ❧   ❧

WHITEFIELD'S "SOUL-TRAP."

The present Whitefield's Tabernacle, on the west side of the Tottenham Court Road, is the third building that occupied the site since the great George Whitefield preached here. The original chapel, irreverently called White-field's Soul-Trap, was built in 1756 on ground leased from Captain Fitzroy. The original foundation-stone, laid by Whitefield, has its place in the present building. He preached the opening sermon from the text, " Other foundation can no man lay than that is laid, which is Jesus Christ."

❧

Whitefield was his own architect, but he had no sooner finished the building than Queen Caroline, consort of George II, took a hand in the design. Riding past the chapel one day, she observed that a great number of people were being turned away, and not liking to see smoking flax quenched at such a rate, she sent Whitefield a sum of money with which to enlarge the building. This he immediately did by clapping an octangular annexe on its front. In this curious building Whitefield thundered the gospel to audiences which included such distinguished figures as the Prince of Wales, Lord Chesterfield, David Hume, Horace Walpole, Garrick, and such oddities—half converts and half scoffers—as Tate Wilkinson and Ned Shuter. The secret of his power was his abandonment. An actor by talent, he overcame his audiences by the variety of his appeals. His maxim was " to preach, as Apelles painted, for Eternity." He had never forgotten a remark made to him by Dr. Delany, who said : " I wish whenever I go up into a pulpit to look upon it as the last time I shall ever preach, or the last time the people may hear." Every sermon of Whitefield's was like a ninth wave. Tate Wilkinson, who could imitate his manner to the life, used to give this specimen of his preaching habit :—

I am told that people say I *bawl*. Well, I allow it, I *do* bawl, and I *will* bawl—I will not be a velvet-mouthed preacher. I *will not* speak the word of *Gud* in a drowsy manner, like your church preachers—your *steeple-house* preachers. I'll tell you a story.

The Archbishop of Canterbury, in the last age, was acquainted with Betterton, the player. You all have heard of Betterton. One day the Archbishop of Canterbury said to Betterton the player, " Pray inform me, Mr. Betterton, what is the reason you actors on the stage can affect your congregation with things imaginary as if they were real, while we of the church speak of things real, which our congregations only receive as if they were imaginary ? " " Why, my Lord Archbishop (says Betterton the player), the reason is very plain. We actors on the stage *speak* of things imaginary as if they *were* real, and you in the pulpit *speak* of things real as if they *were* imaginary." Therefore, I will bawl, I will *bawl.* I will not be a velvet-mouthed preacher.

♣

Garrick said of Whitefield that he could make men weep or tremble by his varied utterances of the word " Mesopotamia." He thrilled Hume with awe when, with uplifted hands and eyes aflame, he cried, " Stop, Gabriel ! stop. Gabriel ! stop ere you enter the sacred portals, and yet carry with you the news of one sinner converted to God ! " These and similar effects were used by him again and again in his sermons with no diminution of effect. He would indulge in the most daring burlesques and familiarities, and trust to his power of controlling his audience. Thus he would end a sermon by saying, " I am now going to put on my condemning cap. Sinner, I must do it. I must pronounce sentence on you." He would pause, and then like a whirlwind came the words, "*Depart from Me, ye cursed, into everlasting fire, prepared for the Devil and his angels.*" Occasionally he would overshoot the mark, and dissolve his audience in laughter which he could not stop. Foote, whose libels on Whitefield in " The Minor " were disgraceful, had some excuse for his remark that the preacher of Tottenham Court Road was " like the cow—after giving a good pailful of milk he was apt to kick it down again."

♣

Whitefield proposed to lay his bones in the vaults of his favourite Tabernacle, and he told his congregation, " Messrs. John and Charles Wesley shall also be buried here. We will all lie together." But they were all buried elsewhere, only Mrs. Whitefield was laid in the vaults of the Tabernacle. Yet even her remains and those of all other persons, except Augustus Toplady, the author of the hymn " Rock of Ages," have been removed to Chingford Cemetery. The old Tottenham Court Road graveyard of the chapel is now one of the County Council's playgrounds. A story is told of it. Whitefield could not get the ground consecrated in the orthodox way, so he had a cartload of top soil brought from one of the City churchyards

and sprinkled over the ground. With this skin-
deep consecration he was satisfied. The feet
of children now patter on the asphalt over the
resting-places of Whitefield's flock.

♣ ♣ ♣

A STATUE THAT WAITED.

A London statue that took one hundred and
eleven years to erect is something out of the
way. The equestrian effigy of William III in
St. James's Square was first proposed in 1697.
No more was heard of it until 1724, when one
William Travers left a legacy to defray its cost.
In 1735 a pedestal appeared in the garden of
the square. It remained vacant for seventy
years, during which the money earned dividends
which nobody claimed. When their existence
was discovered they were used to commission
the present statue by John Bacon, the younger.
It is of brass, and was set up in 1808.

♣ ♣ ♣

DANIEL LAMBERT.

Inasmuch as a writer no less distinguished
than George Meredith describes London as
" the Daniel Lambert of cities " it is proper to
give a place in this gallimaufry of London anecdote to the man whose corpulence could suggest

57

such a phrase. The " Dictionary of National Biography " admits Lambert to its pages as " the most corpulent man of whom authentic record exists." On Ludgate Hill, close to St. Paul's, stands a tavern which bears his name.

♣

Daniel Lambert was born in Leicester in 1770, his father being the Keeper of the gaol. He was apprenticed to a button-engraver in Birmingham, and as a youth was active in sports. It was when he was nineteen that his future greatness began to be foreseen by himself or his friends. On his father's resignation of his post at the prison Lambert succeeded him, and his bulk forthwith increased rapidly. He is said to have been a humane gaoler, and on his discharge in 1805, under a scheme of reorganisation, he was awarded a pension of £50. Meanwhile he had become sublimely corpulent. In 1793 his weight had been thirty-two stone, but it was now a little over fifty stone. It was suggested that he should exhibit his fifty stones.

♣

His reluctance to do so was overcome, and in 1806 he came to London. For the journey he had a carriage specially constructed, and in it he arrived at his lodgings at No. 53, Piccadilly.

From the first he was liked and respected by his visitors, though he had sometimes to snub them. After exhibiting himself for five months, Lambert returned to Leicester. He came to London again in 1807, and gave receptions in Leicester Square. He died at the Waggon and Horses Inn, at Stamford, on July 21st, 1809, and was buried in St. Martin's burial-ground, Stamford. "His coffin was six feet four inches long, four feet four inches wide, and two feet four inches deep." This coffin, which consisted of 112 superficial feet of elm, was built on two axletrees, and four cog wheels. Upon these his remains were rolled into his grave, which was in a new burial-ground at the back of the church.

♣　　　♣　　　♣

A WANDERING STATUE.

The fine statue of James II which stands in the new Admiralty grounds at the east end of the Mall has had a curious history. It is the work of Grinling Gibbons, and represents this monarch of unhappy memory in the dress of a Roman Emperor. The material of the statue has been variously described as lead, brass, and bronze. Actually it is bronze, and it is known that its cost was £500, which expense was borne by Tobias Rustat, a wealthy man, who started life as apprentice to a barber-surgeon, but whose taste for Court employment led him into the service of three successive Kings of England.

♣

Many Londoners will remember this interesting statue in its old place, in the middle of Whitehall Yard, behind the Banqueting House. There it had stood for more than two hundred years. A baton held in the right hand of the monarch is missing. Its removal gave an odd and mistaken significance to the monarch's outstretched forefinger, which was said to be pointing to the spot on which Charles I had been beheaded. This, however, was all imagination. (Charles was executed against the Whitehall front of the Banqueting House.) In 1898 the statue was removed from the seclusion of Whitehall Yard to the garden of Gwydyr House, facing Whitehall.

The inscription on the low pedestal is as follows:—

JACOBUS SECUNDUS
Dei Gratia Angliæ Scotiæ,
Franciæ et Hiberniæ rex.
Fidei defensor.
Anno MDCLXXXVI.

Then came the Coronation of Edward VII, and the space on which the statue stood was required for spectators of the great pageant. James II was again deposed. Wrapt in a tarpaulin and thrust into a corner, he waited until King Edward had gone by. Finally, his much-travelled effigy found its present site.

♣   ♣   ♣

BENJAMIN FRANKLIN AS A "DRY" LONDON COMPOSITOR.

Benjamin Franklin lived in London at various periods; the house in Craven Street, where he lived as the agent of the American colonies, is marked with a tablet. He probably always retained an affection for the Lincoln's Inn Fields district, where he worked at Watts's printing works in Wild Court as a compositor. There his fellow printers dubbed him the "American Aquatic" because he drank water at his meals, their own consumption of beer being, according to Franklin, not less than five pints a day per man. But they recognised young Franklin's brain-power, and allowed him to revise the laws of their chapel. They borrowed money from him with such regularity that the table on which the weekly wages were paid was also the table on which they settled with the "Aquatic." Franklin's landlady was the widowed daughter of a Protestant clergyman who had married a Catholic and become one herself. She and Franklin vied in frugality; "half an anchovy, a small slice of bread and butter each, with half a pint of ale between them, furnished commonly their supper," from which it appears that B. F. was not wholly "aquatic."

♣　　♣　　♣

THE OLD ADMIRALTY SEMAPHORE.

The Marconi apparatus on the roof of the Admiralty building, in Whitehall, is one of the most fascinating objects in London. Through that delicate web of wires Britain speaks to her war-captains around her coasts and for many hundreds of miles to sea. But these Marconi masts have but taken the place of telegraph wires which, again, had superseded the old hand-worked semaphore by which, in Nelson's day, messages were sent from roof to roof and hill to hill until at Portsmouth they reached the quarter-decks.

♣

What a sight for a London boy must have been those mysterious rising and falling shutters whose message was understood in the station at St. George's Fields and was at once transmitted to the next point of observation! As late as 1841 such a boy watched them spell-bound; his name was George Augustus Sala. Dickens, one imagines, must often have seen this predecessor of the telegraph during his dreary years in the blacking warehouse hard by. The rapidity with which messages could be sent down from the Admiralty to Portsmouth or Deal seems incredible. It is said that under favourable conditions, the expert signallers could convey a message all the distance in less than a minute.

❧

There were twelve stations between London and Plymouth, eight of which were part of the Portsmouth line, the separation taking place in the New Forest. Another chain of nineteen stations extended from London to Yarmouth. The route between London and Portsmouth was as follows: The Admiralty—Chelsea—Putney—Kingston—Cooper's Hill—Chatelly—Pearly—Bannick—Haste—Holder—Beacon—Compton Down—Portsdown Hill—Southsea Beach—High Street, Portsmouth. The distances between the stations on all the lines averaged about eight miles.

❧

For a graphic picture of the working of these

B 2

interesting naval signals one may turn to Sir Richard Phillips's gossipy book " A Morning's Walk from London to Kew " (1820). That worthy bookseller and alderman stayed, in his " Walk," to examine very thoroughly the signalling station, and he describes this old system in detail. He states that the number of signals provided was sixty-three—" by which they represent the ten digits, the letters of the alphabet, many generic words, and all the numbers which can be expressed by sixty-three variations of the digits."

There may still be men living who have seen these primitive telegraphs at work. As late as 1909, Professor Walter W. Skeat communicated to *Notes and Queries* his recollection of seeing the semaphore signal on One Tree Hill, near Peckham, in operation. This was about 1843 or 1844.

♣   ♣   ♣

THE SPREAD OF LONDON.

St. George's Fields, on which, from the Middlesex side of the Thames three bridges rapidly converge, are now the bricky threshold of the great Elephant and Castle centre, and have lost every vestige of their old rural and playground character. As long ago as 1795 a stone on the Goldsmiths' Arms in this district was naïvely inscribed:—

> Here Herbs did grow
> And Flowers sweet,
> But now 'tis called
> Saint George's Street.

A summary of London's growth that could hardly be bettered.

♣   ♣   ♣

LONDON MISNOMERS.

This skit on the street names of London was by James Smith, brother of Horace Smith and, with him, joint author of the brilliant parodies contained in " Rejected Addresses."

From Park Lane to Wapping, by day and by night,
    I've many a year been a roamer,
And find that no lawyer can London indict,
    Each street, ev'ry lane's a misnomer.
I find Broad Street, St. Giles's, a poor narrow nook,
    Battle Bridge is unconscious of slaughter,
Duke's Place cannot muster the ghost of a duke,
    And Brook Street is wanting in water.

I went to Cornhill for a bushel of wheat,
    And sought it in vain ev'ry shop in,
The Hermitage offered a tranquil retreat,
    For the jolly Jack hermits of Wapping.

Spring Gardens, all wintry, appear on the wane,
    Sun Alley's an absolute blinder,
Mount Street is a level, and Bearbinder Lane
    Has neither a bear nor a binder.

No football is kicked up and down in Pall Mall,
    Change Alley, alas ! never varies,
The Serpentine river's a straitened canal,
    Milk Street is denuded of dairies.
Knightsbridge, void of tournaments, lies calm and still
    Butcher Row cannot boast of a cleaver,
And (tho' it abuts on his garden) Hay Hill
    Won't give Devon's duke the hay fever.

The Cockpit's the focus of law, not of sport,
    Water Lane is affected with dryness,
And, spite of its gorgeous approach, Prince's Court
    Is a sorry abode for his Highness.
From Baker Street North all the bakers have fled,
    So, in verse not quite equal to Homer,
Methinks I have proved what at starting I said,
    That London's one mighty misnomer.

These lines must not be considered as more than a *jeu d'esprit*, for although many London street names have had curious or obscure origins, and many others have been corrupted, it would be hard to find one that was an original " misnomer." Battle Bridge (now represented by Battle Bridge Road, St. Pancras) was apparently named after a real battle, possibly one between Alfred and the Danes, possibly between

Boadicea's Britons and Suetonius Paulinus. Duke's Place (Aldgate) has its name from Thomas Howard, Duke of Norfolk, beheaded in 1572. Spring Gardens was named after an actual spring, not the season; and Brook Street after the Tyburn Brook. Mount Street took its name from " Oliver's Mount," a mound which figured temporarily in the line of fortifications constructed by order of Parliament in 1643. Hay Hill never had to do with hay: the name refers to the Eye or Aye brook, another name for Tyburn Brook. The Cockpit is referred to in another section of this book and its transformation explained. The origin of " Bearbinder's Lane " which, in the form of " Berebyndereslane," is found as early as 1341, seems to be obscure; this lane is now George Street, behind the Mansion House. The bakers had never " fled " from Baker Street, which was named after a Sir Edward Baker.

♣   ♣   ♣

OLIVER CROMWELL'S HEAD.

Oliver Cromwell's head has long been supposed to be in existence, and to be the embalmed head now, or formerly, in the possession of the Rev. H. R. Wilkinson. This gentleman delivered an address on the subject at the Royal

Archæological Institute in March, 1911, when he exhibited the head to his audience. A public discussion followed, and strong opinions for and against the authenticity of the relic were delivered. Sir Henry H. Howorth and Dr. Boyd Dawkins, both eminent antiquaries, declared the skull to be indubitably Cromwell's. Describing the effect of Mr. Wilkinson's lecture, Dr. Dawkins said: " It is impossible not to accept this as the real head of the great Protector, the man to whom England owes so much."

What, then, if we should live to see the solemn re-burial of Oliver Cromwell's head in Westminster Abbey! A *re*-burial it would be. Cromwell's first burial was in the Abbey, where the site of his tomb is marked to this day by a slab on the bays of Henry VII's Chapel. Here the great Protector was laid with fitting pomp, but, it is said, with little lamentation. Two vivid descriptions of the scene have come down to us. " It was," says Cowley, " the funeral day of the man who late made himself to be called Protector. . . . I found there had been much more cost bestowed than either the dead man, or even death itself, could deserve "; and John Evelyn wrote: " The joyfullest funeral that ever I saw, for there were none that cried but dogs, which the soldiers hooted away with a barbarous noise, drinking and taking tobacco in the streets as they went."

❧

Even at this point legend and dispute creep in, for it is said that the real interment had taken place two months before in private, and this mystery, says Dean Stanley, " probably fostered the fables which, according to the fancies of the narrators, described the body as thrown into the Thames, or laid in the field of Naseby, or in the coffin of Charles I at Windsor, or in the vaults of the Claypoles in the parish church of Northampton, or ' carried away in the tempest the night before.' " A hazy eighteenth-century writer quotes the tradition that Cromwell's mutilated remains were obtained by some of his devoted followers and reverently buried in a field on the north side of Holborn, and that the spot was marked by the obelisk which formerly stood in the middle of Red Lion Square. No credence can be given to this story.

❧

The Royalists were never in doubt that Cromwell had been laid in the Abbey, and at the Restoration they carried out a ghastly disinterment and desecration of his remains and those of Ireton and Bradshaw. It is not to be doubted that the three heads which Londoners became accustomed to see on the roof of Westminster Hall were those of the three " rebels." A Royalist writer described this exposure of the Protector's skull as " the becoming spectacle of his treason." There these heads remained for a generation. Then a strange thing happened. When the Great Storm of 1703 (of which a separate account is given in this book) was raging over London a ghastly object fell from the roof of Westminster Hall. It was the head of Oliver Cromwell. A sentry picked it up and, carrying it home, concealed it during the rest of his life. He made a statement concerning it on his death-bed, and his friends sold the relic to a family named Russell. It is said that Sir Joshua Reynolds had a great desire to purchase the head, which was ultimately sold to James Cox, an antiquarian dealer. Later, the head came into the possession of the Wilkinson family in 1812, under circumstances known and attested.

♣ ♣ ♣

MAJOR FOUBERT'S PASSAGE.

It is now Foubert's Place, but its narrow complexity of old shops and houses, suggesting antiquity, makes an agreeable change from the stony modernity of our new Regent Street. Foubert's Place is on the east side of the street, and leads indefinitely into Soho. In any map of London earlier than 1814 you will find Regent Street represented by Swallow Street, but " Foubert's Passage " may be seen in maps a century and a quarter older. Who was this Foubert?

He was no obscure landlord or builder. Major Foubert fulfilled, in the reign of Charles II, the functions of Domenico Angelo in the reign of George III, and Philip Astley at a later period: he was the fashionable riding-master of the day. On the spot which now bears his name he conducted his academy. He had come from Paris in 1681. This French equestrian was a welcome guest in London. In his diary, under the date December 18th, 1684, Evelyn gives the following description of the exercises practised at this Academy: " I went with Lord Cornwallis to see the young gallants do their exercises, Mr. Foubert having newly rail'd-in a manage and fitted it for the Academy. There were the Dukes of Norfolk and Northumberland, Lord Newburgh, and a nephew of (Duras) Earle of Feversham. The exercises were—1. Running at the ring;—2. Flinging a javelin at a Moor's head;—3. Discharging a pistol at a mark;— and lastly, taking up a gauntlet with the point of a sword; all these perform'd in full speede. The Duke of Northumberland hardly miss'd of succeeding in every one, a dozen times, as I think. The Duke of Norfolk did exceedingly bravely. Lords Newburgh and Duras seem'd nothing so dextrous."

♣

Foubert's seventeenth-century Riding Academy was as fashionable a lounge for the noblemen and sportsmen of the period as Tattersall's is at the present day. When Swallow Street was pulled down to effect the Regent Street improvements, the greater part of this passage, including the Riding School, which had been converted into livery stables, shared the same fate. Nevertheless, an air of quaintness and antiquity pervades the little alley. Samuel Rogers loved it, and said that in his youth it was called, in full, *Major* Foubert's Passage, " and so I should like to see it called still."

♣   ♣   ♣

THE LONDONER WHO WROTE ''ROBINSON CRUSOE.''

In Oldfield Road, formerly Hussey's Lane, at Stoke Newington, may be seen a long stretch (about 120 yards) of venerable brick wall, pierced to-day with back-doors. This is part of the boundary wall of Daniel Defoe's little estate at Stoke Newington. Here he lived from 1709 to 1729, and here he wrote "Robinson Crusoe." Defoe Road covers the site of the house, which has utterly disappeared. But in Church Street several very fine old brick houses are standing which must have belonged to Defoe's neighbours, and round the old church many of those neighbours must be sleeping.

♣

The appearance of the house has been preserved in an engraving which is reproduced, with a plan of the garden, in Mr. Thomas Wright's biography of Defoe. It was a very plain brick mansion with twelve windows looking on Church Street. Tradition says that it was full of strange cupboards, and that the locks and bars in various parts of the house were formidable. There is something in this that consorts with Defoe's secretive and rather uncanny nature. There were stables for Defoe's horses and "chariot." In the garden, which was four acres in extent, he walked and talked. Indeed, behind this brick wall in Hussey's Lane his golden years were spent. A frequent visitor to the house, Henry Baker, the naturalist and founder of the Bakerian lectureship, speaks of his " very genteel ways of living," and declares that his " three lovely daughters were admired for their beauty, their education, and their prudent conduct." Sophia was so pleasing to Mr. Baker that he married her.

♣

Undoubtedly the claim of Stoke Newington to have been the birthplace of " Robinson Crusoe " has been freely challenged. But Lee, in his exhaustive " Life " of Defoe, replies to these stories that Defoe was living in London when his book was published, being then in the pay of the Government, and that " Robinson Crusoe " could have been written only in his own house at Stoke Newington. The fact that Charles Gildon's well-known burlesque dialogue on " Robinson Crusoe," published less than half a year after Defoe's work appeared, laid the scene of that dialogue in a field at Stoke Newington is fairly conclusive evidence.

♣

One would like to think that Defoe had died in peace in the house in which he wrote his one work of genius. This was not to be. He became a discredited politician, and a broken-hearted wanderer. A few months before his death he was a fugitive in Kent, and wrote to Mr. Baker (now his son-in-law) these pathetic lines: " I am so near my Journey's end, and am hastening to the Place where ye Weary are at Rest, and where ye Wicked cease from trouble." The weary old pamphleteer and novelist crept back into London a few months later, and died in Ropemaker's Alley, in Moorfields. They clumsily registered his death thus: " 1731, April 26th. Mr. Dubowe, Cripplegate." He was laid in Bunhill Fields, where, over his grave, there now stands an obelisk subscribed for in 1870 by boys and girls of England.

♣   ♣   ♣

A PRIZE-FIGHTER BURIED IN WESTMINSTER ABBEY.

A prize-fighter buried in Westminster Abbey ! Can this be true? The pugilist in question is no other than Jack Broughton, who is often described as the founder of the British School of Boxing. " Broughton's Rules " were long held sacred in the prize-ring, and are still regarded as the alphabet of pugilistic law.

♣

Born in 1705, Broughton began as a Thames waterman. He made his appearance as a professor of self-defence at George Taylor's famous booth at the " Adam and Eve " at the head of the Tottenham Court Road. There he defeated his master, and was encouraged to set up a larger and more convenient amphitheatre on his own account. Seceding from the Tottenham Court Road establishment, he rapidly built a new prize-ring adjoining the Oxford Road, near the spot where Hanway Street, Oxford Street, now stands, and opened it on March 10th, 1743. From prints in the British Museum, it appears that this building was somewhat similar to Astley's original circus and riding-school in Westminster Road.

♣

To Broughton the Ring owed the introduction of gloves. He thus announced his new invention in the *Daily Advertiser* of February, 1747:—

Mr. Broughton proposes, with proper assistance, to open an academy at his house in the Haymarket, for the instruction of those who are willing to be initiated in the mystery of boxing . . . and that persons of quality and distinction may not be debarred from entering into a course of those lectures, they will be given with the utmost tenderness and regard to the delicacy of the frame and constitution of the pupil ; for which reason mufflers are provided, that will effectually secure them from the inconveniency of black eyes, broken jaws, and bloody noses.

After fighting for several years, and maintaining his ascendancy, Broughton was vanquished by Slack, in April, 1750, at his own Amphitheatre. Some thousands were lost on his unexpected defeat; and nearly £150 was taken at the door, not counting many tickets sold at a guinea and a half each, all of which went to Slack, who is supposed to have gained nearly £600 by his victory. After this defeat Broughton never fought again, and his amphitheatre was shut up. His principal patron and backer, no other than the Duke of Cumberland, lost £10,000 on the contest.

♣

Broughton died, January 8th, 1789, at Walcot Place, Lambeth, in his eighty-fifth year. Although many authorities, including the " Dictionary of National Biography," state that he was buried in Lambeth Church, he almost certainly sleeps peacefully with his wife in the cloister of Westminster Abbey. In this controversy it is well to remember that Broughton, after his retirement from the Ring, filled an honourable place in the Yeomen of the Guard, which he held until his death. There is even ground for believing that in his later years the ex-pugilist was a verger of the Abbey. In Dean Stanley's " Historical Memorials of West-

minster Abbey " it is clearly indicated that
Broughton is buried in the West Cloister. His
burial here is attested both by a wall tablet and
a gravestone in the pavement. Here is the inscription on the wall tablet:—

BENEATH THIS TABLET LIE THE REMAINS OF
MRS. ELIZABETH BROUGHTON.
DIED 7TH DECEMBER, 1784.
AGED 59 YEARS.

ALSO OF MR. JOHN BROUGHTON,
ONE OF HIS MAJESTY'S USHERS
OF THE YEOMEN OF THE GUARD.
DIED 8TH JANUARY, 1789.
AGED 86 YEARS.

The gravestone on the floor is thus inscribed:—

HERE LIETH THE BODY OF
MRS. ELIZABETH BROUGHTON,
WIFE OF MR. JOHN BROUGHTON,
WHO DIED THE 7TH OF DECEMBER, 1784.
AGED 59 YEARS.

MR. JOHN BROUGHTON,

DIED JANUARY 8TH, 1789,
AGED 86 YEARS.

In the second of these epitaphs it will be noticed
that a gap is left after John Broughton's name.
Dean Stanley tells us, on the authority of a
communication made by Broughton's son-in-

law to the master mason of the Abbey, that the gap was intended to be filled by the words " Champion of England." But—" the Dean objected, and the blank remains."

♣

Westminster Abbey may be said to contain a statue of Broughton, for the magnificent figure of Hercules in Rysbrack's monument to Sir Peter Warren in the North Transept was modelled after his gigantic form.

♣　　♣　　♣

THE HERMIT OF CLIFFORD'S INN.

Close to St. Dunstan's Church in Fleet Street, where Dr. Donne, the Dean of all Deans of St. Paul's, was once Vicar, surrounded by the ghosts of the Devil Tavern, Johnson's old Mitre, Nando's coffee house, and Izaak Walton's home in Chancery Lane; ensconced in vestiges and memories, stands that little lagoon of cobbled pavements and red brick walls and wainscoted staircases and casement windows —Clifford's Inn. In its hall Sir Matthew Hale presided over a commission to settle disputes about boundaries arising out of the Great Fire of 1666. The fire stopped just short of Clifford's

Inn, or it might never have become the home of Charles Lamb's eccentric friend, George Dyer.

♣

Dyer lived here for nearly fifty years. His chambers were at No. 13. He was a literary blind-worm who spent all his life in doing a scholar's hack-work. He is said to have contributed all that was original to Valpy's edition of the classics in 141 volumes. His incessant poring over musty books almost destroyed his eyesight, and it was in this way that he became the hero of Charles Lamb's inimitable essay, " Amicus Redivivus." He was without a sense of humour and he would believe any tale that was told to him. On expressing curiosity as to the authorship of the Waverley novels, he was assured by Lamb, in strict confidence, that their author was Lord Castlereagh, who had just returned from the Congress of Sovereigns at Vienna. Dyer immediately ran off to Maida Hill to communicate the fact to Leigh Hunt, who, he thought, as a professional critic, had a right to know. Dyer wrote poetry, in ten-syllable verse. " To G. D. a poem is a poem," says Lamb, " his own as good as anybody's and, God bless him! anybody's as good as his own; for I do not think he has the most distant guess of the possibility of one poem being better than another." G. D. kept all his presentation copies on his third shelf, where they lay untouched and covered with dust. Lamb gave a copy of his own works to Dyer as a matter of form, and shortly after removed it from the shelf and presented it to his friend, Dr. G——, "who little thought whose leavings he was taking."

***

Perfectly honest, perfectly kindly, G. D. was loved by those who laughed at him most. People thought that Lord Stanhope must have been mad to appoint him one of his executors. Lamb used the occasion to put to him the grave inquiry "whether it was true, as commonly reported, that he was to be made a lord." "Oh dear, no, Mr. Lamb! I could not think of such a thing; it is not true, I assure you." "I thought not," said Lamb; " and I contradict it wherever I go; but the Government will not ask your consent. They may raise you to the peerage without you even knowing it." "I hope not, Mr. Lamb; indeed, indeed I hope not; it would not suit me at all," responded Dyer, and went his way, musing and apprehensive. One friend had a wicked story for Dyer's teasing. "You know, Dyer," he would say in company, "that was before you drowned a woman!" "*I* never drowned a woman!" gasped Dyer. The company were then told that when Dyer was a Baptist minister he had led a woman into the water, pronounced the blessing, and left her there.

♣

In the end Dyer's forlorn state excited the compassion of a Mrs. Mather, whose third husband, a solicitor, had just died in the chambers in Clifford's Inn opposite to Dyer's. She advised him to get someone to look after him, and finally assisted Dyer in his deliberations by proposing to take the office on herself. She married him, and did her duty by him very well. She was vigorous so late as December 7th, 1860, her ninety-ninth birthday, when Henry Crabb Robinson found her in the midst of her household on the top floor of Clifford's Inn.

♣   ♣   ♣

DOGGETT'S COAT AND BADGE.

The race for Doggett's Coat and Badge is due to be rowed on August 1st of every year by Thames watermen. The course is from

London Bridge to Chelsea. The race is managed by the officers of the Fishmongers' Company, and has been regularly rowed since its foundation by Thomas Doggett, the Drury Lane actor, in 1716. The custom is to row a number of trial heats in order to reduce the competitors to the convenient six young watermen, who, having passed out of their apprenticeship during the past year, are allowed to row. These six are competitors for the trophy.

♣

Thomas Doggett, the founder of the race, cut a good figure as a man, an actor, and a sportsman. He made his first appearance on the Dublin stage, having been born in that city about the year 1676. As a boy-actor he was tempted to try his fortune in London. From the gala booths of Bartholomew Fair he made his way to Drury Lane, where he is known to have acted in 1691. Colley Cibber testifies in his " Apology " that he became " the most original, and the strictest observer of Nature of all his contemporaries; he borrowed from none of them, his manner was his own." He was greatest in old men's characters, and even in his twenties was playing these regularly. In politics he was a stout Hanoverian, and on

August 1st, 1716, he showed his devotion to the new royal house by issuing the following notice:

This being the day of His Majesty's happy Accession to the Throne, there will be given by Mr. Doggett an Orange Coloured Livery, with a badge representing Liberty, to be rowed for by Six Watermen that are out of their time within the past year. They are to row from London Bridge to Chelsea. It will be continued annually on the same day for ever.

This is the race which, for more than two hundred years, has excited the emulation of young Thames watermen.

A portrait of a waterman in the Watermen's Hall, St. Mary's Hill, is supposed to represent the first winner of the coat and badge. The badge, representing the white horse of Hanover, is painted on the backboard of the boat. It is said that the first race was won by Broughton, afterwards the prize-fighter and the founder of modern boxing. Broughton found a grave in the cloisters of Westminster Abbey, and that story is told a few pages earlier. Under Doggett's will only the coat and badge were given, but supplementary prizes have been added under the will of Sir William Jolliffe and by the Fishmongers' Company. The prizes are modest, but even the last young waterman to reach the winning post (he must reach it) is sure of £2; the other four unsuccessful ones receive from £3 to £4 each; while the winner is £10 in pocket and wears the COAT.

♣   ♣   ♣

FROM ST. JAMES'S STREET TO WATERLOO.

Among the London dandies and worldlings of the Regency, no man had more quiet depth and talent than Captain Rees Howell Gronow. Returning in 1814 from the Peninsula with his regiment, the 1st Foot Guards, he became one of the most popular figures in clubland, at Almack's, and in all the best assemblies. He knew everybody and went everywhere. He was utterly correct where correctness was needed, yet had more than a touch of eccentricity.

♣

One who knew Gronow well (M. H. de Villemessant) describes him as a small, natty man who spent his days seated at his club window, sucking the knob of his gold-headed cane, and watching the fashionable crowd. Yet he was a soldier to his finger-tips. Not Brummell's ties, not Alvanley's wit, not Byron's talk, not Catalina's songs, not Wattier's dinners, could detain him from the wars. When Wellington was at Brussels in 1815, and Gronow found himself left ingloriously in London with the 2nd Battalion of the Guards, his soul rose above parades and discipline. He begged a friend to intercede for him to Sir Thomas Picton, who was going to Brussels with his aides-de-camp. Picton said that the " lad " might come with him if he could obtain leave. Gronow had no leave, nor money for his outfit. He went to Cox and Greenwood, the military bankers, and borrowed £200. Then he took this inadequate sum to a gambling-house in St. James's Square and won £600 in an evening. Having purchased two superb horses at Tattersall's and all his paraphernalia, he embarked for Ostend. Even now he had not obtained leave, but he calculated that he would see the great battle and return in time to mount guard at St. James's.

♣

The party sailed from Ramsgate, and arrived at their destination the same evening. The great Picton at once began a flirtation with a pretty waiting-maid in the Ostend hotel. A day or two later they were all breakfasting at Brussels when Picton was summoned by the Duke of Wellington, who was in the park walking with Fitzroy Somerset and the Duke of Richmond. Gronow, whose position was entirely anomalous, was advised to look up his own regiment. He did so, and the officers received him with shouts of " What the deuce brought you here? Why are you not with your battalion in London? Get off your horse and explain how you came here! " But it was no time for snubbing a young man.

♣

The measured boom of artillery was heard, and the immortal British squares were forming. Napoleon's white horse could be descried through field-glasses. Gronow's fate was settled by the adjutant, who said: " As he is here, let us make the most of him; there's plenty of work for every one. Come, Gronow, you shall go with Captain Clements and a detachment to the village of Waterloo, to take charge of the French prisoners." " What the deuce shall I do with my horse? " Gronow asked. Upon which Captain Stopford, aide-de-camp to Sir John Byng, volunteered to buy the animal. Having thus become a foot-soldier, Gronow started for Waterloo. He lived through the thick of the fight to pen a brilliant description of the battle, in which the sucker of cane-knobs writes: " I shall never forget the strange noise our bullets made against the breastplates of Kellermann's and Milhaud's cuirassiers, six or seven thousand in number, who attacked us with great fury. I can only compare it, with a somewhat homely simile, to the noise of a violent hailstorm beating upon panes of glass."

♣ ♣ ♣

THE MARQUIS OF GRANBY.

Much of London's history might be written from a study of its inn-signs, particularly of those which indicate what national heroes successively swayed the hearts of Londoners. Each had his day, but taverns have a way of enduring in spite of moral crusades and restrictive laws: it is therefore still possible to verify in the streets of London the truth of the old lines:—

Vernon, the Butcher Cumberland, Wolfe, Hawke,
  Prince Ferdinand, Granby, Burgoyne, Keppel, Howe,
Evil and good have had their tithe of talk,
  And fill'd their signpost then, like Wellesley now.

♣

The Marquis of Granby certainly enjoyed as much, or more, of popular and public-house favour than the most resounded of the poet's heroes. His fame has been further extended by the adoption of the sign by Dickens for Mr. Tony Weller's snug little tavern at Dorking, where unhappily his wedded comfort was interfered with by the intrusions of Mr. Stiggins.

88

Here we are concerned only with the fact that the " Marquis of Granby " at Dorking, like almost any " Marquis of Granby," displayed on its sign-post " the head and shoulders of a gentleman with an apoplectic countenance, in a red coat with deep blue facings, and a touch of the same over his three-cornered hat, for a sky."

The Marquis was himself no stranger to a good tavern, and according to Peter Cunningham he spent many an hour at the once famous Hercules Pillars public house, in Piccadilly, where Fielding's Squire Western baited his horses when in pursuit of Tom Jones. It is said that the first " Marquis of Granby " tavern was opened at Hounslow by a discharged soldier of the Horse Guards named Sumpter. The Marquis was Colonel of the Horse Guards from 1758 till his death twelve years later, when a poet asked,

What conquests won will Britain boast,
  Or where display her banners ?
Alas ! in *Granby* she has lost
  True courage and good *Manners*.

Henry Angelo, who knew the hero as a visitor to his father's celebrated riding-school in Soho, says: " I recollect his portrait hanging on a sign-post near Chelsea College, close upon the spot which the renowned Wilkie has since chosen for his picture, which will immortalise himself and those chosen heroes of Waterloo." He adds that the day was when Granby's " fine bald head was seen swinging at as many ale-house doors as that of the fat Duke of Cumberland, in his gold-laced hat, or King Charles in the royal oak." The Marquis lived at Kensington House, and Angelo declares that long after his death a pair of jackboots which he wore at the battle of Minden hung in a colon-nade near the entrance of the house, and that he had often seen them " on looking over the wall from the top of the Bath coach."

♣   ♣   ♣

A GRAVE IN BAYSWATER.

A solemnising grave is to be seen in the dis-used burial-ground of St. George's, Hanover Square, situated in the Bayswater Road, oppo-site Hyde Park, and surrounded by fine streets. A more startling place than this vast field of the dead it is difficult to imagine. Who would suppose that such a Golgotha lay behind the fair frontages of these great houses, or that it was to be entered through a door at the side of that unique resting-place for wayfarers, Mrs. Russell Gurney's Chapel of the Ascension, where the stillness and beauty of pictures invites to meditation? Yet so it is. The burial-ground is exactly square, and of an area almost equal to Lincoln's Inn Fields. All it offers to the eye is a vast, almost treeless expanse within four enclosing walls of immense length, against which are placed innumerable bleached gravestones. Without special guidance one's hope of finding a required stone is small, but there is no missing the grave of Laurence Sterne, the unhappy, whimsical, and inimitable author of "Tristram Shandy."

&

It is on the west side of the enclosure, under a plane tree, and stands out a few yards from the wall. It has both a headstone and a footstone. But whether Sterne's bones really lie there is doubtful. A ghastly story is sufficiently indicated in this passage from Leslie's "Life of Sir Joshua Reynolds": "The graveyard lay far from houses; no watch was kept after dark; all shunned the ill-famed neighbourhood. Sterne's grave was marked down by the body-snatchers, the corpse dug up, and sold to the Professor of Anatomy at Cambridge. A student present at the dissection recognised under the scalpel the face." The remains are said to have been brought back to St. George's burial-ground—an improbable story on the face of it—but whether they were replaced in the same spot is not certain. The inscription on the stone reads:—

ALAS! POOR YORICK.
NEAR TO THIS PLACE
LYES THE BODY OF
THE REVEREND LAURENCE STERNE, A.M.
DYED MARCH 18TH, 1768.
Ah! Molliter Ossa quiescant.

Here follows a eulogy in verse, followed by a statement that the headstone was erected by "two Brother Masons," for "although he did not live to be a Member of this Society, yet all his incomparable Performances evidently prove him to have acted by Rule and Square." The footstone, with an inscription showing the care now taken of the grave, was erected by the present owner of the Sterne property in Yorkshire.

♣   ♣   ♣

"NOSEY."

The traditional London theatre gallery cry, "Play up, Nosey," had its origin in an incident related by Captain Grose in his entertaining "Olio."

Cervetti, the famous player on the violoncello, so well known at the Drury Lane Theatre by the nickname of "Nosey"—bestowed on him in reference to his big nose—was one night the recipient of a violent blow on that organ from a potato thrown from the upper gallery. Cervetti, who was very popular, asked to be shown the scoundrel who had assaulted him, and, the man being pointed out, he seized him by the collar, dragged him into the passage, and gave him a good drubbing.

♣

Some years later, in returning from a ride, he met near Paddington a cartload of convicts going to their execution at Tyburn. One of the prisoners, seeing him, cried out "Nosey! Nosey!" and on his telling the mob that he wished particularly to speak to Nosey, Cervetti was stopped, and his horse led up to the fatal cart. He at once recognised the man who had thrown the potato. The unhappy criminal told him that, being just about to leave the world, he was anxious to die in peace with all mankind: he therefore had taken the liberty of stopping him, to ask his forgiveness for the offence he had formerly given him, and to assure him that he, on his part, had forgiven the beating he had then received. Then, wishing " Nosey " good-day, he bade the carter drive on.

♣　　♣　　♣

THE OLD CHELSEA BUN HOUSE.

Chelsea was long famous for its buns and bun-shops. In 1711 Dean Swift wrote to Stella: " Pray, are not the fine buns sold here in our town; was it not *R-r-r-r-r-r-r-r-r-are Chelsea buns?* " He adds that he had just bought one, and found it stale: the Dean was unlucky, for it was not on stale buns that four generations of the Hands family built up their wealth and reputation. King George the Second and his Queen are said to have frequented the Bun House; as well as George the Third and Queen Charlotte, when their children were young. The second Queen presented Mrs. Hands with a large silver mug, with five guineas in it, as a mark of her approval of the attentions shown to her, which mug was long preserved by the family.

♣

It is unnecessary to say that Good Friday was a great day at the Old Chelsea Bun House. A writer in the *Mirror* (1839) states: " During

94

the prosperous times of the late Mrs. Margaret Hands, upwards of £250 have been taken on a Good Friday for buns, the making of which commenced more than three weeks before the day of sale, in order to prepare the necessary quantity; they were kept moist, and re-baked before being sold. During the palmy days of Ranelagh, the Bun House enjoyed a great share of prosperity, which fell off upon the close of that establishment, and it continued to decline under the management of the late occupier, a Mr. Loudon who had succeeded the Hands family, notwithstanding it appears that he sold, on last Good Friday, April 18th, 1839, upwards of 24,000 buns, which were compounded of eight sacks of fine flour, butter, sugar, and new milk, the sale of which produced upwards of £100."

In his " Book for a Rainy Day " John Thomas Smith reproduces an old Chelsea Bun House announcement, which shows that Good Friday occasionally brought more trade than Mrs. Hands desired. It is said that as many as fifty thousand people would assemble here on a Good Friday morning; finally, on this account Mrs. Hands ceased to make and sell hot cross buns, but her " Chelsea " buns remained as famous as ever. Of the good quality of these buns there can be no doubt. A local poet testified:—

There's a charm in the sound which nobody shuns,
Of smoking hot, piping hot, Chelsea Buns!

Sir Richard Phillips, in his " Morning's Walk from London to Kew," says that he never passed the Chelsea Bun House without filling his pockets with buns whose " delicate flavour, lightness, and richness have never been successfully imitated."

♣ ♣ ♣

THE STRANGE DEATH OF FRANCIS BACON.

On the wide green lawn of Gray's Inn Gardens, under the shade of the great plane trees in which the rooks built not long ago, there are two old catalpa trees which are believed to have been planted by Francis Bacon during his residence in the Inn as its treasurer. It is certain that the gardens were laid out and planted with trees during his term of office. Tradition says that many of the older trees were planted by him; but those versed in forestry are dubious. The catalpa trees are, however, almost certainly of Bacon's planting, and everything is done to preserve them.

♣

If they could talk, they might fill out that

fine picture of London's past which is thrown upon the mind's eye by Sir Walter Raleigh's statement to Sir Thomas Wilson: " I had a long conversation with him (Bacon) in Gray's Inn walks." What makes this conversation so interesting is that it took place just after Bacon had been made Lord Keeper, and just before Raleigh sailed on his last hapless voyage—when both men were on the eve of decline and misfortune. Often must Bacon from his rural exile at Gorhambury, and Sir Walter from his plague-struck flotilla at the mouth of the Orinoco, have looked back on that quiet talk on the sward of Gray's Inn, and the young catalpas' white blossoms.

♣

On a sunny but bitterly cold March day in 1626 Bacon rode from Holborn to Highgate, his mind running on certain experiments concerning " the conservation and induration of bodies." At Highgate, acting on an idea, he jumped out of his carriage, on an impulse, to try the effect of snow in preserving flesh from putrefaction. With this object he called at a cottage and bought a fowl, whose crop he there and then stuffed with snow. While performing this not very pleasing experiment he caught a chill, and felt its effects so immediately that he was unable to return to Gray's Inn. In this fix he bethought him of the Highgate home of his friend, the Earl of Arundel, and thither he was carried.

♣

The Earl was absent, but his housekeeper and servants paid the illustrious guest every attention. From his bed, and ignorant of his approaching end, Bacon dictated a letter to his absent host, informing him of what had occurred, and thanking him for the hospitality he had taken as granted. His letter ended: " I know how unfit it is for me to write to your lordship with any other hand than mine own; but in troth my fingers are so disjointed with this fit of sickness that I cannot steadily hold a pen." Bacon never did hold a pen again. He died there, of bronchitis, on Easter Sunday, April 9th, 1626.

♣　　♣　　♣

GARRICK'S FAREWELL TO THE STAGE.

After having held the town for quite twenty years as the supreme master of the theatre, David Garrick made up his mind to retire. He had achieved the height of his ambition—and thought to say Good-bye. There are many stories about Garrick—about his meanness, his generosity, his faults and follies—but all historians are agreed upon one point, and that is his goodness of heart. He remembered his early days, and he gave with a free hand.

♣

Mrs. Clive, who tried to persuade herself that she hated Garrick, was one night standing at the wings, weeping and scolding alternately at Garrick's acting. Angry at last at finding herself so affected, she turned on her heel, crying, " D— him, he could act a gridiron." Garrick was the best hated, and perhaps, by some who knew him well, the best loved and admired man of his time. The supercilious, and ever the insincere, gossiping Horace Walpole would not, or perhaps could not, see the qualities of his supreme tragic and comic powers in the characters he rendered into life. For he was equally great as a tragedian and as a comedian. According to the best authorities, he excelled in all parts and, despite the carpers and the jealous, he was able to fill Drury Lane Theatre every night he played. He retired at the height of his theatrical glory. There was no lagging superfluous on the stage. He felt that he wanted rest after his long and triumphant career, and when his farewell performances were announced the theatre was crowded night after night. On the last night of all, fearing the emotion that a tragic performance might create, he played the comedy part of Don Felix in " The Wonder." The vast audience looked at him with lingering rapture, and his last words were said through tears.

♣

On the previous night there had been a touching scene. He played Lear to the Cordelia of Miss Younge. As the curtain descended, they lay on the stage together hand in hand, and hand in hand they rose and went, Garrick silently leading to his dressing-room; whither they were followed by many of the company. " There stood Lear and Cordelia, still hand in hand, and mute. At last Garrick exclaimed, ' Ah, Bessie, this is the last time I shall ever be your father; the *last time*,' and dropped her hand. Miss Younge sighed, too, and replied affectionately, with the hope that before they finally parted he would kindly give her a father's blessing. Garrick took it, as it was meant, seriously, and as Miss Younge bowed her head,

100

he raised his hands, and prayed that God would bless her! Then, slowly looking round, he murmured, ' May God bless you all ! ' "

♣ ♣ ♣

STORM, SERMON, AND SIMILE.

Rather more than twenty years ago, when the Kingsway-Aldwych improvement was in progress, the London County Council's crowbars were at work on a little old chapel which some Londoners will remember in Little Wild Street, Drury Lane. This dingy old chapel had for nearly two hundred years been famous for its connection with the GREAT STORM which devastated England in November, 1703. The effects of this storm on land and sea were so dreadful that a public fast was observed throughout the country, and an annual service of thanksgiving, and of allusion to the dire event, was kept up year by year in Little Wild Street Chapel. An annual sermon had been instituted by a Mr. Joseph Taylor, a member of the Baptist Church meeting in Little Wild Street, who sought in this way to commemorate his own merciful preservation during the tempest.

♣

For many years these sermons were regularly printed, but this practice was discontinued in 1821. They were still duly announced and preached however about thirty years ago. The bills announcing them commonly took the following form:—

GREAT STORM.

On Sunday Evening, November 27th, 1825, The

𝔄nnual 𝔖ermon

In commemoration of the Great Storm in 1703, will be preached

In Little Wild Street Chapel,

Lincoln's Inn Fields,

By the Rev. Thomas Griffin,

of Prescott Street.

Service commences at half-past six o'clock.

The storm spread death and havoc everywhere, and some of its worst effects were felt in London. It killed the Bishop of Bath and Wells and his wife; it killed Lady Penelope Nicholas, sister to the Bishop of London—in each instance by the fall of buildings. Two thousand stacks of chimneys were blown down in London. The damage in the City alone was computed at nearly two millions. Many people believed that the war of the elements was accompanied by an earthquake. In the Thames any number of ships were driven down stream, and over five hundred wherries were lost.

♣

In the sermons preached in Little Wild Street

these happenings were frequently recalled, possibly with embellishments. Of "special providences" there were hundreds. A house in the Strand, containing fourteen persons, collapsed, and no one was hurt. In Poultry two boys were lying in a garret. A huge stack of chimneys falling in made their way through their floor, and all the other floors down to the cellar, followed by the bed with the boys in it, who awoke in the nether regions quite unhurt. Narratives like this go far to explain the popularity of the Little Wild Street sermons.

♣

It is an interesting fact that this storm made the fortune of no less a literary genius than Joseph Addison. Sidney Godolphin, whose position as Queen Anne's Tory Minister was none too firm, bethought him that what the Tories needed was a stronger representation in literature. He questioned Lord Halifax, who, after some uncertainty, mentioned Addison. The result was " The Campaign," and the famous simile of the Angel riding the whirlwind. Wishing to glorify Marlborough's generalship, it occurred to Addison to recall the storm which, after nine months, still haunted the public imagination. He did so in the following lines, which not only won him the warmest favour of Godolphin, but captured the admiration of the whole country:—

> So when an angel, by divine command,
> With rising tempests shakes a guilty land
> Such as of late o'er pale Britannia past,
> Calm and serene he drives the furious blasts
> And, pleased the Almighty's orders to perform,
> Rides in the whirlwind, and directs the storm.

Before the poem had been out many days, Addison was appointed to a commissionership worth £200 a year, and from that date his rise to much higher emoluments was assured. He took his rightful place in the world of rank and fashion; and in the Haymarket, where he had been a lodger up three pairs of stairs, he now filled his tortoise-shell snuff-box at Fribourg and Treyer's, whose quaint bow-windowed shop stands unaltered to this day.

♣　　♣　　♣

"THE COUNTRY COUSIN'S LITTLE COMMISSIONS TO HER COUSIN IN LONDON."

A great deal of humour used to be extracted from the "country cousin's" ignorance of London. To-day "country cousin" is an almost obsolete phrase, but it is amusingly vivid in the following verses dating some seventy or eighty years back. At that time one Ebenezer Flint kept for some forty years a very well-known

drapery shop near the corner of Ludgate Hill and Far-
ringdon Street, just where the railway bridge now spans
the roadway:—

Dear Cousin, I write this in haste,
　To beg you will get for mamma
A pot of best jessamine paste,
　And a pair of shoe-buckles for pa,
At Exeter Change;—then just pop
　Into Aldersgate Street for the prints;
And while you are there you can stop
　For a skein of white worsted at Flint's.

Papa wants a new razor strop,
　And mamma wants a Chincilli muff;
Little Bobby's in want of a top,
　And my aunt wants six-pen'orth of snuff;
Just call in St. Martin's-le-Grand
　For some goggles for Mary (who squints);
Get a pound of bees'-wax in the Strand,
　And the skein of white worsted at Flint's.

And while you are there you may stop
　For some souchong in Monument Yard;
And while you are there you can pop
　Into Mary-le-bone for some lard;
And while you are there you can call
　For some silk of the latest new tints
At the mercer's, not far from Whitehall,
　And remember the worsted at Flint's.

And while you are there, 'twere as well
   If you'd call in Whitechapel, to see
To the needles; and then in Pall Mall,
   For some lavender-water for me:
And while you are there you can go
   To Wapping, to old Mr. Chint's;
But all this you may easily do
   When you get the white worsted at Flint's.

I send, in this parcel, from Bet,
   An old spelling-book to be bound,
A cornelian broach to be set,
   And some razors of pa's to be ground.
O dear, what a memory have I!
   Notwithstanding all Deborah's hints,
I've forgotten to tell you to buy
   A skein of white worsted from Flint's.

♣   ♣   ♣

THE THAMES STEAMBOATS.

It is an amazing fact that the London's " silent
highway " should have been more useful to
eighteenth and early nineteenth-century Londoners than it is to-day. The last great effort
to run steamboats on the Thames was made
by the London County Council some twenty
years ago. Mr. John Burns, who has most
happily described the Thames as " liquid his-

tory," took a great interest in the scheme, and with characteristic originality he persuaded the Council to change their intention to distinguish these steamboats by the cold device of numbers by naming them after great Londoners. One hopes that this his happy idea may be brought to life again. The steamers plied under such names as " King Alfred," " Chaucer," " Raleigh," " Shakespeare," " Pepys," " Gibbon," and " Charles Lamb." The boats were large, and were about thirty in number, but they were a dismal failure.

It is well over a century since the first passenger steamboat began to ply on the Thames. It was put there by George Dodd, an assistant of Rennie, the engineer who designed Waterloo Bridge. Built at Glasgow and launched as the " Margery," this pioneer boat was 90ft. in length and 15ft. in beam. Her arrival was the talk of London in the spring of 1815. After a period of river work she was re-christened the " Thames," and turned into a Margate packet. She replaced, in fact, the old sailing hoy, whose disappearance Charles Lamb whimsically lamented. Before 1815 Londoners bound for Margate were frequently becalmed for hours together.

Even the steam-driven " Thames " took twelve hours to make the voyage from London Bridge to Margate.

♣

One of the earliest Thames steamboat services was from Queenhithe to Richmond. The boat picked up passengers from wherries in midstream; and the Cockney of 1826, standing on her decks, saw himself monarch of all he surveyed. Hear a chronicler of the time:—

> He will tell you of the capital porter-shops that were in Palace Yard before the old coffee-houses were pulled down, and he directs you to the high chimney of Hodge's Distillery, in Church Street, Lambeth. . . . At the Red House, at Battersea, he would absolutely go ashore, if his wife and daughters had not gone so far in geography as to know that Richmond is above Battersea Bridge.

The goal of these happy Londoners of 1826 was the Roebuck inn at Richmond.

♣

The steam-packet traffic on the Thames grew so rapidly that in 1836 it was stated in evidence before a Committee of the House of Commons that more than a million passengers were using the boats within the year. The fares were low. Indeed, there were halfpenny boats seventy years ago. Londoners poured down from the

Strand through the Adelphi Arches, before the Embankment days, to catch the little " Bee " or " Cricket " for London Bridge. These boats were very small, and had a rudder at each end. They carried a motley crowd. But boats superior to these " halfpenny " tubs were running and were remunerative. They live for us in the " Endeavour " of the " Sketches by Boz," so vigorously put into commission for a pleasure cruise by Mr. Percy Noakes, law student of Gray's Inn and " devilish good fellow." It was in the " Endeavour," one remembers, that Captain Helves left unfinished his fearsome story of the Gum-Gum.

♣   ♣   ♣

" NUMBER TEN."

There are many thousands of little two-storey, jerry-built houses in the suburbs of London which bear more impressive names than the one from which they and half the world are governed The house in which the British Government reaches its decisions might well bear some august name like Britannia House, Empire House, Constitution House, or Pitt House. Actually it does not rise even to the dignity of a House. It is " a number " in a small street on the west of Whitehall, upon which an estate auctioneer possessing the rhetorical gifts of the celebrated Mr. George Robins (who is said to have described a gallows as a " picturesque hanging wood ") might expend himself in vain. Not that Number 10, Downing Street, is a mean building, but that in appearance it can be matched in many of London's old squares. Its blue-grey brick, neatly pointed, is beyond reproach, but its walls are as other walls and its windows as other windows. The hub of the British Empire might be any rich man's town house.

❧

" Number Ten " was one of four great houses which that strange political adventurer, George Downing, built in what is now Downing Street. Of these only Nos. 10 and 11 survive. The name " Downeing Street " had come into being before its creator died. The story of No. 10 is really that of England in the last two centuries. George I lent the house to Baron Bothmar, the Hanoverian Minister, at whose death it was again at the Royal disposal. Next, George II offered it to Sir Robert Walpole, who refused it as a personal grant, but persuaded the King to allot it as a residence for First Lords of the Treasury. Sir Robert took up his residence in 1735, and from its door a few years later he saw his wife borne to her grave in Westminster Abbey. Here, in an American-built house, Lord North fought America until the day when, hearing of Cornwallis's surrender at Yorktown, he spread his arms and exclaimed: " O God! It is all over!" Here the venerable Earl of Chatham rested after his fainting fit in the House of Lords, before being taken to Hayes Place to die. Here his great son directed our reeling ship of State through the French Revolution and early Napoleonic period, until the day when he cried: " Oh, my country! How I leave my country!"

&

Mr. Gladstone did not want Number Ten, and lent it to his private secretary, Sir Algernon West. In his reminiscences West tells this remarkable story:—

It came one day in 1872 that I was summoned to Downing Street, and on my arrival I was surprised to find Mr. Gladstone in the garden with Sir Henry Storks and Sir Frederick Abel, who had promised to demonstrate the art of felling trees noiselessly by gun-cotton. A mast had been planted in the ground with a necklace of gun-cotton around it, which at the proper time was to be exploded. Mr. Ayrton, then First Commissioner of Works, who was not a scientific believer, was protesting against the experiment, but on Sir Frederick's assurance that nobody would be " one penny the worse," the gun-cotton was exploded with a terrific report, which was heard in Hyde Park. I found myself under a shower of glass, which had fallen from the skylight of the First Lord's house, and all the adjoining windows were smashed.

There was one person who rejoiced—that was the triumphant Ayrton. Theories were exploded as well as gun-cotton.

The house, however, survived, and in 1894 it saw the sunset hour of Gladstone's political life, when he attended his last Cabinet, and after sitting, as Lord Morley tells us, composed and still as marble, made a five minutes' speech of farewell in steady tones, ending with the words, " God bless you all."

And still the great story of No. 10 goes on.

♣ ♣ ♣

THE ONLY PLACE.

London is the only place in which the child grows completely up into the man.

HAZLITT.—" Londoners."

♣ ♣ ♣

" POP GOES THE WEASEL."

This once famous and still unforgotten London song had its birth in the last 'fifties at the Grecian Saloon (or Eagle Tavern) in the City Road. The Grecian replaced an older resort, the Shepherd and Shepherdess (the name is perpetuated to-day in Shepherdess Walk), about the year 1825. Thomas Rouse, founder of the Grecian, was a highly successful provider of public amusement. Under him many popular singers arose, and a few actors who passed to West-end theatres and became famous. His great artists were, Harry Howell and Robert Glindon. Glindon's "Literary Dustman," who

> Took in the Penny Magazine,
> And Johnson's Dixionary,
> And all the Periodicals
> To make him Literary,

is not wholly forgotten, or, for that matter, extinct.

⚜

The Grecian kept revelry at the base of the City Road and White Conduit House at the top. But the Grecian hummed loudest. It was crowded nightly, and attracted a sprinkling of distinguished visitors. One night the gaunt figure of Paganini was seen gyrating in the crowd, and he was so enthusiastically mobbed that he had to retire. Another visitor, not so known to her generation as she is now to posterity, was Miss Jemima Evans, whose exclamations of "How 'ev'nly!" are known to every reader of Boz. Her rhapsodies had reference to the gravelled walks, the refreshment boxes, " painted and ornamented like so many snuff-boxes," and the waiters tearing about with glasses of negus. Her lady friend's " Ancore ! " was echoed by the gentleman in the plaid waistcoat, or an outspoken opinion on Miss Jemima Evans's lady friend's ankles led to sudden war between Mr. Samuel Wilkins and the waistcoat, resulting in the departure of the ladies " in a hackney coach and a state of insensibility, compounded of shrub, sherry, and excitement."

Why did the weasel pop ? And what *was* the weasel ? The explanations offered are learned but diverse. Even if they miss the mark, they all contribute something to the social history of the City Road :—

> Up and down the City Road,
>   In and out the Eagle,
> That's the way the money goes,
>   Pop goes the weasel.

> Every night when I come home,
>   Supper's on the table ;
> That's the way the money goes,
>   Pop goes the weasel.

Obviously the popping of the weasel had a close connection with the going of the money. This lends a superficial probability to the explanation that " weasel " was slang for silver-plate, etc., and that the popping (pawning) of the " weasel " was the corollary of a night's extravagance up and down the City Road. It is also suggested that a " weasel " was more precisely a watch—the wide-awakeness of each object being the link between the animal and the time-keeper.

More abstruse is the theory that a " weasel " was an iron implement used by a tailor in cutting his cloth, and so necessary to him that " popping the weasel " represented the last resource of a man whose cash had gone the night before in drinking negus at the Eagle and listening to such provocative ditties as " Nothing Like Wine." A similar explanation makes " weasel" synonymous with the domestic flat-iron. On top of all this come the erudite remarks of another etymologist, who declares that " weasel " was the dancer, and that "Pop goes the weasel " is really the name of an old English jig that was revived in the 'fifties, and became as fashionable as the cake-walk did later. Indeed, we are told that the dance was advertised to be taught to fashionable folk by " that able professor of dancing, Monsieur Coulon, of Great Marlborough Street, London."

In face of such diversity even the " weasel " must be allowed to sleep.

♣   ♣   ♣

A SMITHFIELD MARTYRDOM.

Although Smithfield is now the hub of one of the coarsest of London's trades, its air is dense with history. Enter it in the quiet of a Saturday or Sunday afternoon and the whole area speaks to you of concourses long disbanded and dramas long played out. One has the sense of a deserted amphitheatre. When Londoners look into the past of Smith field, with its Bartholomew Fair and its more ancient jousts and tournaments (of which the memory is preserved in the name of Giltspur Street), they see little but the smoke of the Marian burnings which have made " Smithfield " a synonym of persecution. It is too much forgotten, however, that while Catholic Mary burned Protestants here, Protestant Elizabeth burned Anabaptists, and that there were burnings in Smithfield before Mary and after Elizabeth.

♣

One of the most pitiful was that of Anne

Askew, at the close of the reign of Henry VIII. The tragedy was enacted in front of the old gateway of the Priory. In the first edition of " Foxe's Book of Martyrs " there is a remarkable wood-cut. The scene it delineates is good for the whole series of martyrdoms: the balefully neat circle of spectators, the executioners collecting their faggots within it; the Priory Tower; the platforms and awnings reserved for the Prior and the officers of state and law. For denying the Real Presence in the sacrament, Anne Askew had been several times examined, and had been racked in the Tower. It was necessary to carry her to Smithfield, where, chained to the stake, she listened with critical attention to the sermon preached to her and two fellow-sufferers by Dr. Shaxton, who had held her own views but saved himself from her fate by recantation.

❧

The like means of escape was now offered to Anne Askew by Lord Chancellor Wriothesley, who sat among the officers under the Priory wall. She replied that she had not come there to deny her Master. The Lord Mayor muttered his " Fiat justitia," and the flames burned toward the gunpowder which was the last mercy granted to this frail and fearless woman. She was burned on an autumn day, and this circumstance prompts one historian to remark that " the ground must have been black with the ashes of that Christian heroine, over which the dogs danced, and the Devil in the miracle play jested not many days later at Bartholomew Fair."

♣   ♣   ♣

LONDON'S RECALL.

I'm sick for London again; sick for the sounds of 'er, an' the sights of 'er, and the stinks of 'er; orange peel and hasphalte an' gas comin' in over Vauxhall Bridge. . . . That an' the Stran' lights, where you knows ev'ry one.

RUDYARD KIPLING: STANLEY ARTHERIS *loq*.

♣   ♣   ♣

WHERE TURNER DIED.

The hand of England's greatest landscape painter, Joseph Mallard William Turner, R.A., had weakened, and his spirit had become clouded, after 1845. He had grown weary of his great gloomy house in Queen Anne Street, in which many of his most glorious pictures were going to ruin from dust and damp; and he sought relief from disgust, and a better air, in Chelsea, where his old friend Tom Girtin had painted his beautiful picture " The White House," and where he had himself painted his first exhibited picture, the "Moonlight at Millbank."

☙

Turner's discovery of his river-side cottage in Cheyne Walk, Chelsea, was an odd business. One morning the landlady found on her door-step a little thick-set, shabby man who wanted rooms. She asked for a "reference," and he replied, testily, "My good woman, I'll buy the house outright." Then she wanted an agreement, but Turner merely showed her a roll of bank-notes. And thirdly she wanted his name, and received the reply, "Name, name, what is *your* name?" "My name is Mrs. Booth." "Then I'm Mr. Booth." However it came about, Turner soon became known in Cheyne Walk and thereabouts as "Puggy Booth" by the boys, and as "Admiral Booth" by the tradesmen. He seems to have had a liking for disguises and assumed names in his latest years. To Mayall, the Strand photographer, in whose work he took a keen interest, he had once contrived to suggest that he was a Master in Chancery!

☙

For a considerable time the great painter was lost to his friends. If they ever saw him he contrived to evade their questions about his new residence. Determined to be alone and at

119

peace, Turner did not even communicate his address to his faithful old housekeeper at Queen Anne Street, Mrs. Danby, whose anxiety grew as time passed. One day she was brushing one of his old coats when she found in a pocket a letter which gave her a Chelsea clue. With another old lady, as infirm as herself, she went there on an expedition of search. A conversation with a ginger-beer seller confirmed Mrs. Danby's suspicions: Turner was living in the cottage close by, but had not been seen for some time, and was thought to be ill. He was so ill, indeed, that he died next day, December 19th, 1851.

To the last he clung to life, shadowed and lonely though it was. He had sent to Margate for a doctor who had formerly treated him, and in whom he had confidence. He came, and his first biographer, Thornbury, thus describes the end:—

The dreadful, despairing fear of annihilation pressed upon the heart of this great man, who had done so much to make men love God's beautiful world.

The old painter died with the winter morning sun shining upon his face as he was lying in his bed. The attendant drew up the window-blind, and the morning sun shone on the dying artist.

The little house in Cheyne Walk stands to-day, hardly altered since Turner knew it. Some say that it was he who placed the guarding railing on its roof, where he stood sketching the river, the Battersea shore opposite, and the slow moving boats and barges, others that it was there originally, and attracted Turner by its convenience.

♣ ♣ ♣

THE DEMON BARBER OF FLEET STREET.

The legend of Sweeney Todd, the Demon Barber of Fleet Street, lodges in the minds of many Londoners. They have at least heard the story named, and its title is rather convincing. You have surname and nickname, occupation, and address; and you have the thrilling word " demon " to invest all these with a stimulating horror. No doubt a great many uneducated Londoners do believe that Sweeney Todd used to tip his customers down a trap-door into his Fleet Street cellar, which was said to be connected with the mutton-pie shop next door. As a writer in *Notes and Queries* has delicately remarked: the gist of the legend lies in the statements that some of the barber's customers were never seen to emerge from his shaving establishment, and that the pie-maker was never known to buy mutton.

♣

The story has interest from several points of

view. Seventy or eighty years ago, and for long afterwards, it had a gruesome charm for potmen and servant girls; it was developed into a long tale and issued in various publications, and separately; and it was staged at several theatres, where it was seen by cultured students of London life. Dickens did not disdain to refer to the story. It will be remembered that Tom Pinch after his giddy arrival in London, and while walking with John Westlock, " was particularly anxious, among other notorious localities, to have those streets pointed out to him which were appropriated to the slaughter of countrymen." The reference becomes more precise in the chapter in which we are assured that " Tom's evil genius did not lead him into the dens of any of those preparers of cannibalistic pastry, who are represented in many standard country legends as doing a lively retail business in the Metropolis."

♣

Thus the legend could be alluded to by Dickens in 1843 in general terms, with the certainty of the allusion being understood. Yet it was then not more than about twenty years old. And here we come to the curious fact that this well-rooted Fleet Street legend was nothing but an importation from Paris. In 1823 its first English version had appeared in a monthly journal called the *Tell-Tale*, published by Henry Fisher. It was then offered frankly as " A Terrific Story of the Rue de la Harpe, Paris," and it described the murder by a Paris barber of a country gentleman for the sake of a casket or string of pearls. The barber was said to have disposed of the body to a pie-maker, whose pastries were highly popular. Other " awful discoveries " went to enrich the tale. It seems possible that Dickens had the Sweeney Todd legend in mind when he put into the mouth of Sam Weller the story of the fate of the inventor of the " patent-never-leavin-off sassage steam engine " which turned Mr. Pickwick pale.

    ♣   ♣   ♣

THE WESTMINSTER BRIDGE ECHO.

The stone alcoves which were placed along either side of old Westminster Bridge (Labelye's fine structure, built in 1739) provided a curious echo for the delectation of Londoners. A writer of the period tells us : " So just are their proportions, and so complete and uniform their symmetry, that, if a person whispers against the wall on the one side of the way, he may be plainly heard on the opposite side; and parties may converse without being prevented by the interruption of the street or the noise of carriages."

♣

In 1904 "Londoner," then in his seventy-third year, wrote: "I often sat in these alcoves as a boy, and on one occasion my father bade me sit in one while he went to one opposite. I could distinctly hear his voice through the noise of the traffic, although he was speaking in an ordinary tone. My father told me that this remarkable carrying of the sound had led to the discovery of a murder. I remember a play being produced on the Surrey side called, I think, 'The Mystery of the Murder on Westminster Bridge.' The echo of the alcoves was the leading idea, and there was a flaming poster showing the murderer sitting in the alcove." This Westminster Bridge was weakened by the increase of the river's flow caused by the removal of London Bridge, and was replaced by the present bridge in 1862. Several of the old stone alcoves can be seen to-day in Victoria Park.

♣　　♣　　♣

SIR WALTER RALEIGH AT ISLINGTON.

"Merry Islington" was little more than a hamlet in Queen Elizabeth's time. The Islington fields were then the great playing-fields for Londoners, and the archery grounds to which citizens came out to shoot with the long-bow—though even in the reign of Henry VIII the rich had begun to enclose the fields, and it had needed the cry of " Shovels and Spades! " and a great horde of London apprentices, armed with these implements, to level the hedges and fill the ditches. At this period the village consisted of a few farmhouses; but it was not till the seventeenth and eighteenth centuries that Londoners flocked to the Islington dairies for the creams, custard cakes, and gooseberry fool for which the place was famous.

※

One of the greatest of Englishmen—scholar, traveller, soldier, courtier, poet—chose Islington to build himself a house. He returned to it here after the glitter of courts, rested here after the fierce turmoil of discovery and adventure, studied here, wrote here, and smoked here some of the first tobacco ever smoked in England; for Islington was at one time the home of Sir Walter Raleigh. His house was still standing there in 1830, when it was pulled down. Prints of it were published after it had become the Pied Bull Inn and grown dilapidated, but it retained traces to the end of having been a comfortable mansion. The site of the Pied Bull Inn is behind the present Frederick Street.

♣

The old smoking story of Sir Walter has been told in connection with his Islington home. " Sitting one day, in a deep meditation, with a pipe in his mouth, he inadvertently called to his man to bring him a tankard of small ale; the fellow, coming into the room, threw all the liquor into his master's face, and running downstairs bawled out, ' *Fire! Help! Sir Walter has studied till his head is on fire, and the smoke bursts out of his head and nose!* ' It is added that after this affair Sir Walter made his newly-acquired habit no secret, and that he took two pipes just before he went to be beheaded." The sign-post of " Sir Walter Raleigh and his Man," depicting this anecdote, used occasionally to be seen over tobacconists' shops. It was in 1583 that Raleigh introduced tobacco into England, and a few years later smoking-houses were as common in London as beer-houses.

♣   ♣   ♣

THE HIGHGATE OATH.

A century ago the custom of " Swearing on the Horns at Highgate " was described as more honoured in the breach than the observance.

Yet as late as 1865 John Timbs wrote: "The old custom of swearing-in at Highgate continues to this day, and each of the older public-houses keeps the horns ready." More than half a century has passed, and the horns are still preserved in Highgate taverns. In 1826 there were no fewer than nineteen houses, in or about Highgate, where the oath was administered. There is little doubt that the first scene of the ceremony was the Gate House, which still flourishes. The explanation of the custom is that Highgate was the nearest place to London at which drivers and their cattle, bound for Smithfield, put up for the night. As they could not exclude strangers who like themselves were travelling on their business, they instituted this ritual as a test of good-fellowship and to assert their peculiar claim to accommodation. The horns used at the various inns were stag's, bullock's, and ram's. Bullock's horns were used at the Red Lion and Sun whose landlord, Mr. Sontho, was long remembered as " a most facetious swearer-in."

So noted was the Highgate ritual that in 1824 a new landlord of the Fox and Crown, who ignored it, found that his custom fell off. He decided to repair his error, and to carry out the ceremony in future with special pomp. Robed in a domino, with a wig and mask, and holding a book containing the terms of the oath, he recited his part with much gravity, while an old villager interpolated " Amens " at every pause. His performance is the subject of a drawing by George Cruikshank. It remains to describe the ceremony, and this will be best accomplished in the words of one who saw it. The horns were fixed on a pole about five feet in height and held near the person about to be sworn, who in common with everyone present was bidden to take off his hat.

♣

The landlord then addressed him in these searching terms:—

Take notice what I now say unto you, for that is the first word of your oath—mind *that!* You must acknowledge me to be your adopted father ; I must acknowledge you to be my adopted son. If you do not call me father, you forfeit a bottle of wine ; if I do not call you son, I forfeit the same. And now, my good son, if you are travelling through this village of Highgate, and you have no money in your pocket, go call for a bottle of wine at any house you think proper to go into, and book it to your father's score. If you have any friends with you, you may treat them as well ; but if you have money of your own, you must pay for it yourself. For you must not say you have no money when you have ; neither must you convey

the money out of your own pocket into your friends'
pockets, for I shall search you as well as them ; and if it
is found that you or they have money, you forfeit a bottle
of wine for trying to cozen and cheat your poor old ancient
father. You must not eat brown bread while you can get
white, except you like the brown the best ; you must not
drink small beer while you can get strong, except you
like the small the best ; you must not kiss the maid while
you can kiss the mistress, except you like the maid the
best—but sooner than lose a good chance, you may kiss
them both. And now, my good son, for a word or two
of advice. Keep from all houses of ill-repute, and every
place of public resort for bad company ; beware of false
friends, for they will turn to be your foes, and inveigle
you into houses where you may lose your money and get
no redress ; keep from thieves of every denomination.
And now, my good son, I wish you a safe journey through
Highgate and this life. I charge you, my good son, that
if you know any in this company who have not taken
this oath, you must cause them to take it, or make each
of them forfeit a bottle of wine ; for if you fail to do so,
you will forfeit a bottle of wine yourself. So now, my
son, God bless you ! Kiss the horns, or a pretty girl if you
see one here, which you like best, and so be free of Highgate.

♣

If a female was in the room, she was usually
saluted; if not, the horns had to be kissed. As
soon as this salutation was over, the swearer-in
commanded " Silence ! " and then addressing
himself to his new-made son, said : " I have
now to acquaint you with your privilege as a

freeman of this place. If at any time you are going through Highgate, and want to rest yourself, and you see a pig lying in a ditch, you have liberty to kick her out and take her place; but if you see three lying together, you must only kick out the middle one and lie between the other two. God save the King!"

That was the Highgate Oath. What a people we are!

♣   ♣   ♣

"OLD Q" IN PICCADILLY.

In the first ten years of the last century James Douglas, fourth Duke of Queensberry, was regarded as a sort of figure-head of vice, and a cautionary landmark of Piccadilly. Leigh Hunt's description of him is famous, and has been frequently quoted. It may not be a very fair portrait, but it is a portrait: " In the balcony of No. 138, Piccadilly, on fine days in summer, used to sit, some forty years ago, a thin, withered old figure, with one eye looking on all the females that passed him, and not displeased if they returned him whole winks for single ones. This was the Most Noble William Douglas, Duke, Marquess, and Earl of Queensberry."

♣

" Old Q.'s " claims to be called " Most Noble " were many, for he bore five imposing and complicated titles, but his claim to be called respectable has been much disallowed—by no one more strongly and picturesquely than Leigh Hunt, who continues: " He had been Prince of the Jockies of his time, and was a voluptuary and a millionaire. ' Old Q.' was his popular appellation. He died at the age of eighty-six. We have often seen him in his balcony,

> Sunning himself in Huncamunca's eyes,

and wondered at the longevity of his dissipation and the prosperity of his worthlessness. Stories were told of his milk baths, his inhaling the breath of dairymaids, and his getting up interludes of Paris and the Golden Apple, the part of Paris by himself. The last, it seems, was true. His dying bed was covered with *billets-doux;* that is to say, with love-letters addressed (as Molière has it) ' to the sweet eyes of his money-box.' "

≗

This portrait may be overdrawn, but other writers can be quoted in general support of its truth. Thomas Raikes, the dandy and diarist, describes " Old Q." as sitting at his upper bow-window, or balcony, in Piccadilly, scanning the people who passed by, while his groom, Jack Radford, waited on horseback below to convey any message or invitation to anyone who interested him. He adds: " He was one of the last noblemen to keep a running footman. Once, when he was about engaging one, he made the man put on his livery and run up and down Piccadilly. The Duke watched the proceedings from his balcony, and called out: ' That will do; you will suit me very well.' The fellow answered: ' And so your livery does me,' and then ran off, and was never heard of again."

" Old Q." died at last on December 23rd, 1810. He has in recent years found a moderate defender in Mr. Arthur Irwin Dasent, who, in his " Piccadilly During Three Centuries," compares him with Charles II. " Neither of them, at any rate, made vice appear offensive or virtue ridiculous. . . . The ' Merry Monarch ' was only fifty-four at the time of his death, and had ' Old Q.,' in his turn, died at sixty-five instead of eighty-six, his dissipations would never have attracted the notice that they have done."

♣

More interesting is Mr. Dasent's remark that somehow or other " Old Q.," lucky in most of his sports and undertakings, never had the supreme good fortune to meet the right woman at the right time. He made love honourably to Lady Mary Coke, then a young widow. She boxed his ears, but remained his friend. He had already sought an alliance with Miss Frances Pelham, daughter of the Prime Minister, and stuck to his suit with much enterprise for seven years without winning his Rachel. Lady Harriot Stanhope and Lady Susan Stewart also disappointed him, and so did Miss Gertrude Vanneck, daughter of Sir Joshua Vanneck, his neighbour both in Piccadilly and in Richmond. Failing to win love by asking, he " bought it ready-made " (his own expression) in less exalted spheres.

♣   ♣   ♣

THE FIELD OF THE FORTY FOOTSTEPS.

The great cleared site behind the British Museum on which London University may yet find its home was formerly meadow land and known as Montague Fields, from the circumstance that the land lay behind Montague House, the town house of the third Baron Montague, built in 1679. Seven years later this mansion was destroyed by a disastrous fire, in which many art treasures were lost. The Duke erected a second Montague House, where he and his son, the last Duke, were residents until 1749. The Government then purchased the house in order to establish in it the British Museum. Just a hundred years later Montague House was razed to the ground, and the present great British Museum buildings cover its site.

※

In the last quarter of the seventeenth century, and the first half of the eighteenth, Montague Fields were frequented by duellists, and the new London University, if it rises here, may cover the ground which was long known as the Field of the Forty Footsteps. The precise spot to which the mysterious forty footprints drew Londoners in their walks hereabouts has been disputed, but the margin of difference is very slight. Robert Hill, the water-colour painter, who lived long in the neighbourhood, wrote in a letter, which has been preserved: " I well remember the *Brothers' Footsteps*. They were near a bank that divided two of the fields between Montague House and the New Road [now Euston Road], and their situation must have been, if my recollection serves me, what is now Torrington Square." These footsteps were said to have been visible as late as 1800, when Bloomsbury was beginning to cover the fields. In that year Joseph Moser, the artist, author, and magistrate, wrote in his Commonplace Book under June 16th: " Went into the fields at the back of Montague House, and there saw, for the last time, the Forty Footsteps; the building materials are there to cover them from the sight of man."

The story behind all this melodrama is that at about the time of the Monmouth Rebellion two brothers fought to the death in these fields for the hand of a lady, who sat on a bank and watched them spill each other's blood until both fell to rise no more. Tradition said that the place where this engaging young woman sat, and the footprints made by the two swordsmen, never produced grass again. It was a fine story for Cockney lovers to gloat upon. They trod piously in the footsteps and shuddered. Even the poet Southey was sufficiently interested to seek them out. He found them about five hundred yards east of Tottenham Court Road. But by this time the forty had become seventy-six, according to his count, and he gravely quoted and concurred in the opinion that " the Almighty has ordered it as a standing monument of his great displeasure of the horrid sin of duel-ling."

LONDON TALK.

Whoever has once experienced the full flow of London talk, when he retires to country friendships and rural sports, must either be contented to turn baby again and play with the rattle, or he will pine away like a great fish in a little pond, and die for want of his usual food.

DR. JOHNSON.

♣ ♣ ♣

THE WILD LORD CAMELFORD.

Many old Londoners can remember—by its boundary wall at least—the retired, almost hidden house which stood at the corner of Park Lane and Oxford Street. To this house, which at a later period was the home of Princess Charlotte in her soon-ended married life, was brought the body of Thomas Pitt, Lord Camelford, on a March day in 1804. He had been killed in a duel with his old naval comrade, Mr. Best, which was fought in a field behind Little Holland House in Kensington. It was a sorry affair, and it terminated the career of a brilliant but ungovernable man.

♣

The quarrel which led to Lord Camelford's death was as foolish as it could be. It came to his ears that his friend Captain Best had spoken disparagingly of him in a certain quarter. He went, in a passion, to the Prince of Wales's Coffee House, and seeing Best, said in a loud voice:

" I find, sir, that you have spoken of me in the most unwarrantable terms." Mr. Best replied that he was unconscious of having deserved such a charge. Lord Camelford retorted angrily, and called his friend " a scoundrel, a liar, and a ruffian." A meeting was immediately proposed for the following morning; each having appointed his second, it was left to them to fix the time and place.

That evening Mr. Best wrote to Lord Camelford that the information he had received was unfounded, and that as he had acted under a false impression, he would be satisfied if he would retract the expressions he had employed. This Lord Camelford refused to do. The duellists and their seconds met early on the morning of March 7th in a coffee-house in Oxford Street, where Best said: " Camelford, we have been friends, and I know the unsuspecting generosity of your nature. Upon my honour you have been imposed upon. Do not insist on expressions under which one of us must fall." Lord Camelford replied: " Best, this is child's play; the thing must go on." The mad folly of the duelling system was never more clearly displayed, for when Lord Camelford spurned this offer of reconciliation he knew himself to be in the wrong. He even put the fact on record, for before going to meet his reluctant antagonist he inserted these words in his will: " In the present contest I am fully and entirely the aggressor, as well in the spirit as in the letter of the word; should I therefore lose my life in a contest of my own seeking, I must solemnly forbid any of my friends from instituting any vexatious proceedings against my antagonist."

♣

Camelford fired first, and missed. Then he fell to Best's bullet. The seconds, together with Mr. Best, ran to help him, when he seized his friend by the hand, saying, " Best, I am a dead man: you have killed me, but I fully forgive you." The dying man was carried into Little Holland House, where he lingered till Saturday evening. An inquest was held, at which the jury permitted themselves to return a verdict of wilful murder against " some person or persons unknown." Captain Best was indicted, but the bill was thrown out by the grand jury.

♣

Yet this wild London lord was something better than he may appear; he had read widely, and had a strong taste for science and mathematics. A curious light is thrown on his character by the wish he expressed for his burial. In his travels he had once seen a beautiful spot in Switzerland, in the canton of Berne. Here he desired to be laid. " I wish my body," he said, " to be removed as soon as may be convenient to a country far distant—to a spot not near the haunts of men, but where the surrounding country may smile upon my remains." The spot he had in mind was on the borders of Lake St. Lampierre, and was marked by three trees. The centre tree was to be taken up and there he would rest. From Little Holland House the body was taken to Camelford House, and thence to a vault in the Church of St. Ann, Soho, where it was to await removal to Switzerland. But it has never left that vault in Wardour Street. War prevented the journey to Switzerland, and at last the coffin was bricked up.

♣   ♣   ♣

VOLTAIRE AND THE EAST WIND.

It is difficult to think of Voltaire, the cynic, the iconoclast, the champion of the rights of Reason, in London. As a young exile he landed at Greenwich on a May morning just two hun-

dred years ago. It is probable that Greenwich
fair was in progress, for the first spectacle that
met his eyes was a racecourse and a vast con-
course of people. It was a cloudless day, and
he was intoxicated by the lovely climate and by
the air of liberty which he breathed. He wrote
afterwards:—

I fancied that I was transported to the Olympian
games ; but the beauty of the Thames, the crowd of vessels
and the vast size of the City of London soon made me
blush for having dared to liken Elis to England. I was
told that at the same time a fight of gladiators [a prize-
fight, no doubt] was in progress in London, and I immediately believed myself to be among the ancient Romans.
A courier from Denmark, who had arrived that morning,
and who was fortunately returning to Denmark the same
evening, was beside me during the races. He seemed
overpowered with joy and astonishment ; he believed
that the entire nation was always gay, that all the women
were sprightly and beautiful, and that the sky of England
was always pure and serene.

♣

There is a vein of banter here, and Voltaire
goes on to tell how next day he found everyone
morose, and murder abroad; the wind was in
the east. Greatly astonished by this change in
the manners of the people he inquired of a Court
doctor, who told him that he had nothing to be
astonished at, and that in November and March,
if he stayed, he would see people hang themselves

by the dozen—the wind being then in the east. In those months, the doctor told the astonished Frenchman, " Everyone looks stern and cross, and is disposed to form desperate resolutions. It was precisely in an east wind that Charles I was beheaded and that James II was dethroned. If you have any favour to ask at Court, never go to ask it unless the wind is in the west or south." Though much of Voltaire's time was spent in the then rural Wandsworth with his wealthy and generous host Sir Everard Falkener, he is known to have lodged for some time at the sign of the White Peruke, in Maiden Lane, Covent Garden, a by-street which then, as now, was in the midst of London's theatrical life.

♣ ♣ ♣

CHARLES I AT CHARING CROSS.

The finest equestrian statue in London, and the first of its kind ever seen in England, was cast in Charles's lifetime, sixteen years before his execution, to the scene of which it looks so gallantly. Its sculptor was a Frenchman, Hubert Le Sueur, a pupil of the famous Italian artist John of Bologna, who was a friend of Michael Angelo. He came to London about the year 1628, and lived in Drury Lane and also in Bartholomew Close. It was his good fortune to be commissioned by Sir Richard Weston, afterwards first Earl of Portland, to execute this statue. Sir Richard intended it to ornament the gardens of his new house at Roehampton. The terms of the agreement are known, and seem to have been carefully drawn up: Le Sueur was to have £600 for " the casting of a horse in brass, bigger than a great horse by a foot, and the figure of His Majesty King Charles proportionable, full six foot." The time allowed for completion was eighteen months.

❧

But the statue was never set up at Roehampton, and when the Civil War broke out it was seized by Parliament and, after the King's execution, was sold as old metal to a Holborn brazier named John Rivett, who had orders to break it up. The story goes that Rivett produced some pieces of broken bronze to satisfy the authorities that he had fulfilled his contract. In reality he had reverently hid the statue, an act of piety which did not deter honest John from selling bronze knife-handles to Royalists by the hundred as " genuine " relics of the effigy, and also to rebels as souvenirs of their triumph.

❧

In 1660, Rivett produced the statue intact! When it was claimed, with justice, by the Earl's heir Jerome, who had succeeded to the earldom, he refused to give it up, and until 1674 its ownership was undecided. In that year it was presented to Charles II and erected on the spot formerly covered by the original Charing Cross. The sculptured pedestal is not, as was long said, carved by Grinling Gibbons, but by Joshua Marshall, Master Mason to the Crown, whose hand was also seen in the decorative work on Temple Bar. The King's original sword and straps have had to be replaced. On the night of April 13th, 1810, these accoutrements fell from the statue. They are said to have been picked up by a porter of the old Golden Cross Hotel, named Moxam, and given into the charge of Mr. Eyre, a neighbouring trunkmaker, by whom they were made over to the Board of Green Cloth, and were then replaced. Finally they were stolen from the statue either in 1844, when Queen Victoria was on her way to open the Royal Exchange, or, earlier, in the Coronation crush of 1838. Both statements are made.

♣ ♣ ♣

THE RIVER OF DREAMS.

Glide gently, thus for ever glide,
  O Thames! that other bards may see
As lovely visions by thy side

K 2

As now, fair river! come to me.
O glide, fair stream, for ever so,
Thy quiet soul on all bestowing,
Till all our minds for ever flow
As thy deep waters now are flowing.

WILLIAM WORDSWORTH.

♣   ♣   ♣

THE THREE TAILORS OF TOOLEY STREET.

This trio became famous through a derisive allusion by Canning, in the House of Commons. The three tailors had held a meeting in Tooley Street, now the great provisions mart of London, for the redress of popular grievances, and addressed a petition to the House of Commons beginning, " *We, the people of England.*" A circumstantial account of the three tailors was given by a correspondent of *Notes and Queries* more than forty years ago. He stated that the " tailors " were really two tailors and a grocer, named John Grose, of Tooley Street, Thomas Satterley, of Neston Street, and George Sandham, of Bermondsey Street, and the last named was known by the not complimentary nickname " Spinmischief." They were local politicians who took themselves seriously, and according to this authority they drafted their famous petition against the Catholic Emancipation Bill.

This story was promptly challenged by another correspondent, who pointed out that long before their time, and possibly in Shakespeare's day, there was a sign of "We Three" in Tooley Street. It represented two foolish-looking heads —the third was supposed to be that of the passer-by who was looking at them. This does not account for the "tailors," and it is unlikely that this humorous tavern sign was peculiar to Tooley Street.

♣   ♣   ♣

THE QUEEREST STATUE LONDON HAS KNOWN.

The most remarkable story of a London statue, perhaps of any statue, concerns the effigy of Charles II, which Sir Robert Viner compiled —that seems to be the right word—on the site of the present Mansion House, then an open space called the Stocks Market. Being either thriftily inclined, or in a hurry to please his Royal friend, he used for the purpose an immense statue which he had picked up cheap at Leghorn, a work in white marble supposed to represent John Sobieski, the King of Poland, in the act of trampling on a Turk. He had this re-fashioned until the Polish monarch became Charles II, and the wretched Turk Oliver Cromwell. The eloquent result was unveiled on Charles's birthday, May 29th, 1672, and thereafter it rose above the meat and fish stalls of the market for more than sixty years. In 1736, when the Mansion House was being planned, it had to be removed. For more than forty years it lay in a lumber yard, and then the Corporation presented it to one of Viner's descendants. It may still exist, and, if it does, it seems probable that Cromwell still wears the Turk's turban.

♣   ♣

MILITARY EXECUTIONS IN HYDE PARK.

Probably few Londoners dream that Hyde Park has been the scene of military executions. In his voluminous work, " London in the Eighteenth Century," the late Sir Walter Besant drew much curious matter from little-known books, stories, and pamphlets in which we are brought face to face with the times. From these he took stories which no ordinary reader would be likely to meet with. One of these is a poignant account of a State execution in Hyde Park, following the Rebellion on behalf of the Stuarts. The teller of the story found a young woman beside Rosamond's Pond in the south-west corner of St. James's Park. This pond was a great resort of suicides, and the poor young woman was about to drown herself. She had good cause, for her husband was to be shot that morning for fighting under the enemy's flag. The writer did his best to dissuade her, and his narration proceeds as follows:—

Thus we chatted till about eight o'clock,

when I perceived a great party of the Guards under arms, moving slowly towards us. I requested to know where I could see her again. "To oblige you, Sir," answered she, "you may see me to-morrow morning at Islington Church." By this time she plainly saw the Guards, followed by a prodigious crowd of people; then her outcries and lamentations were affecting beyond expression, frequently saying, "My dear, dear William is the occasion of that crowd; they are now going to tear him from me for ever." She instantly ran to them, and I kept as close to her as possible till we came up to the crowd.

To give you a description of this melancholy sight, the Guards were taking five prisoners to execution to Hyde Park to be shot, who were dressed in white, and attended by chaplains, unbraced, and mourning drums dismally beating. Sadness appeared in every part of this scene. Not all the pageantry used at great funerals can for sorrow equal this, where unfortunate men behold their own obsequies. They moved a slow and solemn pace, when my morning acquaintance threw herself at the feet of her beloved William, and distractedly cried,

" William, my dear, my husband, where are you going? They are leading you to destruction. You shall not go with them. Sure they do not mean to shoot my William. The King has not such a man in his Army." The Guards halted a little. William had a fine person. He stooped and kissed his wife, who was still at his feet, and desired her to bear all with patience. They were ordered to march. He bade her adieu, and she was gently taken away, piercing the hearts of her hearers with her cries, saying, " William, William, are you going to leave me? " and then made an outcry of "Murder! Murder!" These were the last words I ever heard her speak.

&

I walked with the Guards to the fatal spot, which was close to Hyde Park Wall. There were five graves and five coffins ready prepared. They were to be shot at the end of their graves. The five who were to suffer spoke about twenty minutes to different persons. After they prayed half an hour they were put on their knees, and their caps drawn down on their faces. . . . Then, I believe, they could be heard, as far as ever human voices were, invoking God for mercy, till the last signal was given, the hasty forerunner of ending their miseries in this life: their faces and breasts were all torn to pieces by the balls, and all dead before they fell.

♣

What makes me so particular about this execution is because they were the first who suffered this way on account of the rebellion.

Next morning I went to Islington Church to meet poor William's wife, according to her promise to me. I walked a considerable time in and about the churchyard, but could not see her. I perceived greater numbers going more hastily into this church than common, which roused my curiosity, which made me also go in. There, in a shell (a thing made like a coffin, but larger, kept on purpose for sudden deaths), did I see the corpse of the unfortunate, but constant, wife of William, who, two hours before, had been taken out of the New River.

♣   ♣   ♣

SALLY IN OUR ALLEY.

This ballad, one of the sweetest founded on London everyday life, was written and composed by Henry Carey, and was first printed as a popular broadside in 1700. There was no real Sally, that is to say no young woman whom the author knew by that name, and probably no particular "Alley" that he had in mind. Nevertheless, the ballad was founded on a real experience which Carey put upon record as follows :—

A vulgar error having prevailed among many persons, who imagine Sally Salisbury to be the subject of this ballad, the author begs leave to undeceive and assure them it has not the least allusion to her, he being a stranger to the very name at the time the song was composed; for, as innocence and virtue were ever the boundaries of his muse, so, in this little poem, he had no other view than to set forth the beauty of a chaste and disinterested passion in the lowest class of life. The real occasion was this: A shoemaker's 'prentice, making holiday with his sweetheart, treated her with a sight of Bedlam, the puppet-shows, the flying chairs, and all the elegancies of Moorfields, from whence proceeding to the farthing pyehouse, he gave her a collation of buns, cheesecakes, gammon of bacon, stuffed beef, and bottled ale, through all which scenes the author dodged them. Charmed with the simplicity of their courtship, he drew from what he had witnessed this little sketch of nature; but, being then young and obscure, he was very much ridiculed by some of his acquaintance for this performance, which nevertheless made its way into the polite world, and amply compensated him by the applause of the *divine Addison*, who was pleased more than once to mention it with approbation.

Such is Carey's account of the unforgettable ballad which begins and ends :—

Of all the girls that are so smart,
 There's none like pretty Sally,
She is the darling of my heart,
 And she lives in our alley.
There is no lady in the land
 Is half so sweet as Sally,
She is the darling of my heart,
 And she lives in our alley.

. . .

My master and the neighbours all,
 Make game of me and Sally ;
And (but for her) I'd better be
 A slave and row a galley :
But when my seven long years are out,
 O then I'll marry Sally !
O then we'll wed and then we'll bed,
 But not in our alley.

♣ ♣ ♣

"A MAN OUT OF ROSEMARY LANE."

Who beheaded Charles I? This question has exercised many inquirers, but the list of persons suspected of the act is so long as to shroud the personality of the headsman. Never was a sinister secret better kept. It was known only to Cromwell and a few of his colleagues, and they were dumb. Cromwell's own name has actually been mentioned, but it is known that he was a spectator of the execution from a window in the palace. The names of Lord Stair, Gregory Brandon, Phineas Payne, and Christopher Allured, Henry Porter, Giles Dekker, and Captain Foxley can also be eliminated for various reasons.

♣

Even then a remarkable series is left. When all the probabilities are examined, one rejects in turn the traditions that would fasten the deed on William Hulet, an Ironside; Hugh Peters; the truculent priest of St. Margaret's, Westminster; William Walker, a soldier and a Sheffield man, who is said to have several times confessed himself the executioner; Colonel Foxe; and Colonel Joyce, who was greatly suspected, and was strongly affirmed by Lilly, the astrologer, to have been the man. One tradition says that Cromwell brought to London a drover from his Huntingdon estates to strike the tragic blow in Whitehall.

♣

There remain the Brandons, father and son. Mr. Philip Sydney, who examined the whole subject some twenty years ago in *The Gentle-*

man's Magazine, dismisses Gregory Brandon, the father, with the remark that he has simply been confused with the son. That is probably the fact. Still, one must take into account the curious communication made by George Selwyn, that arch-student of horrors, to Sir Nathaniel Wraxhall, and recorded in Wraxhall's memoirs. Here the confusion referred to doubtless occurs, but the passage has its own grim interest. Wraxhall says: " Talking to him of the death and execution of Charles I, he assured me that the Duchess of Portsmouth always asserted, as having been communicated to her by Charles II, that his father was not beheaded, either by Colonel Pride or Colonel Joyce; though one of the two is commonly considered to have performed that act. The Duchess maintained that the man's name was Gregory Brandon."

♣

Gregory Brandon was the common hangman shortly before the Whitehall tragedy. He succeeded the celebrated Derrick, referred to by Scott in " The Fortunes of Nigel," and was himself succeeded by his son, Richard, more probably executioner of the King. Most students fix the stigma finally on Richard Brandon. He was nominally a ragman in the once-famous Rosemary Lane, where Rag Fair was held. Rosemary Lane has vanished in recent years in the construction of the northern approach to Tower Bridge. Its trade prestige had passed to Petticoat Lane (Middlesex Street) early in the nineteenth century. Here, only a few months after he had been smuggled away from the scaffold, Richard Brandon died in infamy. He was at all times a man of the loosest morals, and was probably a bigamist. His burial is recorded in the register of St. Mary Matfellon, Whitechapel, in these words:—

1649. June 21st. Richard Brandon, a man out of Rosemary Lane.

To this is added the memorandum: " This R. Brandon is supposed to have cut off the head of Charles I." He died on Wednesday, June 20th, 1649.

     ♣   ♣   ♣

THE BURNING OF OLD DRURY.

" Fire! Fire! Fire! " When this cry rang down from Drury Lane even to the House of Commons where Sheridan, the manager of the theatre, was taking part in a debate, it seemed as though a national calamity was bodied in the words. The rush and roar of the streets of London came to a half stop, and then the traffic was roused to turn and move headlong towards the great glare that filled the skies of the night, as the words " Fire! Fire! " were echoed.

♣

This theatre, the successor of the original house built by Sir Christopher Wren, had been opened in March, 1794, with a great display of Handel's oratorios and the Coronation March. It is a remarkable fact that when Covent Garden Theatre was burning in September, 1808, all the Drury Lane employés had been busily at work on the roof of their house keeping off the fiery flakes which fell in great profusion and caused much havoc. They little dreamt that a similar fate was in store for the house they were protecting. There had been no performance at Drury Lane on the evening of February 24th, 1809, when suddenly the whole neighbourhood of Covent Garden and Russell Street seemed to be ablaze, and so great was the conflagration that it lit up the town for miles.

♣

Charles Mathews was dining with friends in Lincoln's Inn Fields, when a servant rushed in with the news. The party at once hurried to the scene to try to rescue their goods, for Mathews had a collection of wigs (once Garrick's), some had jewellery; and they succeeded in dragging out an enormous chest. Before twelve o'clock at midnight the whole of the structure was in a blaze. "I stood," says James Boaden, "with my boots covered with water, until I saw the figure on the summit (the Apollo) sink into the flames." The fire was, according to the accounts, appalling; everything was destroyed—books, papers, and some costumes; everything save Mathews's wigs and Mrs. Jordan's dresses. Meanwhile at the House of Commons the news of the fire was communicated to the Speaker, and the House unanimously voted an adjournment. Sheridan, however, protested against such an interruption of public business on account of his own or any other private interests.

﹩

He departed, however, in all possible haste, and whilst seeing his own property in flames—for, of course, he was powerless to arrest the destruction—sat down with his friend Barry in a coffee-house opposite to a bottle of port, coolly remarking, in answer to some friendly expostulation, that it was "hard if a man could not drink a glass of wine by his own fireside." That was Sheridan's way. The new theatre was formally opened in 1812 with a prologue written by Lord Byron. In 1831 the familiar Doric portico in Catherine Street and the colonnade in Little Russell Street were added to the building.

♣　　♣　　♣

TO RING THE BELLS OF LONDON TOWN.

Gay go up and gay go down,
To ring the bells of London Town.

Oranges and lemons,
Say the bells of St. Clement's.

Bull's eyes and targets,
Say the bells of St. Marg'ret's

Brickbats and tiles,
Say the bells of St. Giles'.

Halfpence and farthings,
Say the bells of St. Martin's.

Pancakes and fritters,
Say the bells of St. Peter's.

Two sticks and an apple,
Say the bells of Whitechapel.

Pokers and tongs,
Say the bells of St. John's.

Kettles and pans,
Say the bells of St. Ann's.

Old father Baldpate,
Say the slow bells of Aldgate.

You owe me ten shillings,
Say the bells of St. Helen's.

When will you pay me?
Say the bells of Old Bailey.

When I grow rich,
Say the bells of Shoreditch.

Pray when will that be,
Say the bells of Stepney.

I do not know,
Says the great bell of Bow.

Gay go up and gay go down,
To ring the bells of London Town.

18th-Century Nursery Rhyme.

♣   ♣   ♣

MISER AND LANDLORD.

A great deal of Marylebone, Portman Place and Portman Square district, was built by John Elwes, M.P., who had, in consequence, many houses on his hands. To save expense he would live in any one of his houses which happened to be empty, and the moment he had let it he moved into another. Two beds, two chairs, a table, and a poor old woman, were all the movables this great London landlord had to consider. To-day they were in the Haymarket, to-morrow in a Marylebone attic; and their wanderings were too rapid and fitful to be followed.

♣

In his last years Elwes lived in Welbeck Street, with two maidservants. One of these girls all but succeeded in marrying him. He was then reaching his dotage. But every morning, long before it was necessary, he would trot off to Marylebone to superintend the workmen on his new houses, becoming known to the wondering neighbours as " the Old Carpenter." His sight and memory failing him, he sometimes lost himself in the streets, and was brought home by an errand boy, whom he rewarded with a polite bow. He became an automaton with one idea, that of keeping the wealth which he could not even estimate. He would cry out in the night, " I will keep my money, I will; nobody shall rob me of my property." He refused to undress himself, and would be found in bed fully clad, even to his boots, hat, and stick. It is told of him that when he injured his legs by running against the pole of a sedan chair he scouted the expense of an apothecary, but when he was prevailed upon to call one in, he said to him: " In my opinion my legs are not much hurt, so I will make this agreement; I will take one leg and you shall take the other; you shall do what you please with yours, and I will do nothing to mine; and I will wager your bill that my leg gets well before yours." He beat the apothecary by a fortnight.

Elwes died at last without a sigh in his son's house at Marcham, leaving about £500,000.

♣　　　♣　　　♣

LONDON ENOUGH.

When a man is tired of London he is tired of life; for there is in London all that life can afford.　　　　　　　　　DR. JOHNSON.

♣　　　♣　　　♣

HOBSON'S CHOICE.

Up to the year 1810 a fresco might have been seen in the Black Bull Inn, Bishopsgate Street Within, representing an old man in Puritan dress, wearing a large felt hat and a long cloak, with a ruffle round his neck.　He was bearded, and had a grave and honest expression of countenance—a plain and homely man, but he held a hundred-pound bag under his arm, upon which was written "The fruitful mother of a hundred more,"—an indication that he knew how to make money, and was "a thriving man of lawful gain."

♣

This was Hobson of "Hobson's Choice." Thomas Hobson was the official carrier to the University of Cambridge, licensed also to carry letters before the Post Office system was established. His father, also a carrier, had left him the team ware—the cart and eight horses—and he conveyed, besides letters, packages, and sometimes passengers, between his two destinations.

There's few in Cambridge, to his praise be't spoken,
But may remember him by some good Token.

How much of old English life is hidden under the few facts stated above! The Black Bull in Bishopsgate was the accustomed hostelry for Cambridge carriers.

♣

The traffic between London and the University town was very considerable, and Hobson's trade brought him a comfortable competency. He invested his money in the purchase of horses, and is said to have been the first person in the kingdom to let them out on hire. " Observing that the scholars rid hard," says Steele in the *Spectator*, " his manner was to keep a large stable of horses, with boots, bridles, and whips to furnish the gentlemen at once, without going from college to college to borrow." But for the better security of his horses, and to avoid all ground of dispute, Hobson insisted that the horses should be taken in rotation—" the horse nearest the door should start the first in course. This or none," he would say, so that " Hobson's choice " became a cant phrase to indicate no choice at all. It is not at all unlikely that Hobson carried parcels to a certain undergraduate at Cambridge, who by reason of his long brown hair and dark grey eyes and delicate complexion was known as " The Lady," no other indeed than John Milton; and almost the first subject on which this poet (who, later, was to sound the greatest organ-note in our literature) exercised his skill, was Thomas Hobson, the University carrier. And the grave Milton —for Milton was grave, even at Cambridge— indulged in a series of puns on Hobson and his trade. " His wain was his increase," he writes;

" If I mayn't carry, sure I'll ne'er be fetched,"
he makes Hobson say, and adds, " He died for
heaviness that his cart was light."

♣   ♣   ♣

THE BOY IN LONDON.

> . . . At night along the dusky highway, near
> and nearer drawn,
> Sees in heaven the light of London flaring
> like a dreary dawn,
> And his spirit leaps within him to be gone
> before him then,
> Underneath the light he looks at, in among
> the throngs of men.
>
> TENNYSON.

♣   ♣   ♣

THE BEHEADING OF SIR WALTER RALEIGH.

The scene was Old Palace Yard, not as we
know it now, but with houses crowding in and
narrowing it, so that it looked like an ordinary
London street. The great Elizabethan pioneer,
who had the misfortune to live into the reign
of James I, was beheaded here on Michaelmas
day, 1618, two years after the death of Shakespeare. A sad and silent crowd had gathered
to behold the execution of the most brilliant of

the courtiers, soldiers, and adventurers of the previous reign, because on his return from his last voyage to Guiana he had not brought back ship-loads of the gold of El Dorado. Sir Walter Raleigh was now an old man. His health had been broken by long imprisonment, and his heart by the death of his eldest son; but he had the undaunted mien and the ready wit of the days of his prime. An old and devoted friend darted forward to give him the support of his arm as he walked to the scaffold, and was repulsed by the guards. " Prithee, never fear, Beeston," said Raleigh, " I shall have a place."

꙰

When James I came to the throne Raleigh's life became a series of crushing persecutions. It was found possible in the long run to involve him in a charge to depose James and place the Lady Arabella Stuart on the throne. There was no proof of his complicity; but he was sentenced to death, and then, by the King's mercy, as it was called, was sent as a prisoner to the Tower of London, where he remained for fourteen years; and wrote his " History of the World." James liberated him in order that he might go on another search for Manoa, the King putting some of his own money into the venture. Nothing came of it but disaster. There was more fighting with Spaniards, in the course of which Raleigh's son Walter was killed. "My brains are broken," he wrote to his wife; and he was brought back to England a prisoner in his own ship, "to sue for grace of a graceless face."

The grandeur of the man shone forth in his final hour in Old Palace Yard. To the priest who attended him in his last moments he said that he gave God thanks that he had never feared death, and that as to the manner of it, though to others it might seem grievous, yet that he had rather die so than of a burning fever. "This is a sharp medicine; but a safe cure for all diseases," he said, touching the headsman's axe. Trembling with agitation, the executioner shrank from the block. "What dost thou fear?" asked Raleigh. "Strike, man!" But he was still so unnerved that he had to strike twice. "The extraordinary effusion of blood," it has been remarked, "evinced an unusual strength and vigour of constitution." "The head," said his biographer, "after being as usual held up to the view of the people on either side of the scaffold, was put into a red bag, over which his velvet nightgown was thrown, and the whole immediately carried to a mourning coach which was in waiting, and conveyed to Lady Raleigh."

So perished the last of the Elizabethan heroes.

♣   ♣   ♣

WAS MOSCOW BUILT ON LONDON RUBBISH?

Just a hundred years ago an extraordinary story sprang up concerning the rebuilding of Moscow after the destruction of that city on the entrance of Napoleon and his ill-fated army of 1812. At that time immense dust-heaps, the accumulations of years, were tolerated in London, and one of these, a veritable mountain, was situated at King's Cross, opposite what has long been the railway terminus. The story is thus recorded in Mr. Walter E. Brown's valuable "St. Pancras Book of Dates":—

1826.—Immense Cinder Heap, King's Cross, sold to Russian Government for £15,000. This heap is of historical fame. It was sold to the Russian Government for the purpose of rebuilding Moscow. On the site was afterwards built the King's Cross Theatre.

In the same year William Hone mentioned it in his "Every Day Book," with the statement that this mountain of "cinder-dust" was exported to Russia to be made into bricks to rebuild Moscow. Considering that Moscow was at the

166

time, itself, a wilderness of cinders and dust, the statement seems to lack credibility.

♣

This King's Cross dust-heap consisted of every kind of rubbish that had been shot here without conscience for a century and a half, including bones and hop-husks; it was at one time the haunt of great numbers of pigs, who developed the climbing powers of goats in their exploration of its treasures. Contrary, also, to the tradition it is recorded by a Mr. Noble in Pink's " History of Clerkenwell " that his grandfather bought the entire Golgotha, with sixteen small tumbledown houses thrown in, for £500, so that the story that the Russians gave thirty times that sum for the refuse alone must be rejected as an absurdity. But then absurdity is one of the best known preservatives of a tale that will not bear examination, and doubtless to the end of time there will be Londoners whose choicest piece of London lore will be : " Moscow, you know, is built on London rubbish."

♣   ♣   ♣

A PILL-MAKER'S MEMORIAL.

A very familiar object in St. Pancras is the big couchant lion in a Euston Road forecourt almost facing St. Pancras Road. An inscription on the pedestal states that it was erected by penny subscriptions to the memory of James Morison, "the Hygeist." Morison, whose Pills had an immense vogue in this country and on the Continent, came of a good Aberdeen family, and for a time was settled as a merchant at Riga. After "thirty-five years' inexpressible suffering," he decided to be his own doctor, and he evolved the vegetable pill which became so famous that it attained to figurative mention in the literature of the day. It was often referred to by Mr. "Punch," and a *Figaro* cartoon represented the Duke of Wellington taking the Reform Bill in the shape of a Morison Pill while being held down by Lord John Russell and Earl Grey. The "Hygeist" died in Paris in 1840 at the age of seventy, and it was stated that in the last ten years of his life he had paid £60,000 to the British Government for medicine stamps. Not the least interesting of unwritten books on London would be a history of its pill-doctors.

♣   ♣   ♣

THE SECRETS OF HANGING SWORD ALLEY.

Forking upwards to Fleet Street from the lower end of Whitefriars Street, this alley of the sinister name leads you through a deep ravine of newspaper buildings. Its name belongs to the annals of that strange region which sprang up on the ruins of the great Carmelite priory whose cloisters, guest-halls, gardens, orchards, and cemetery were spread over all the river slope below Fleet Street and have left us the name of Whitefriars Street. When the priory fell, its old rights of sanctuary survived, and were even confirmed to debtors. These unfortunates were joined by rascals of every colour, and for two centuries " Alsatia " remained one of the social sores of London. Macaulay says that even the warrant of the Chief Justice of England could not be executed in its alleys unless backed by a file of musketeers.

To-day Hanging Sword Alley recalls that dangerous rookery. Yet its name is not so dark and reminiscent as it sounds. Stow knew it in Shakespeare's day, and he explains it simply as derived from the sign of the Hanging Sword.

♣

Still, in Hanging Sword Alley stood the notorious Blood Bowl House, whose interior is the subject of Plate 9 in Hogarth's " Industry and Idleness." Tom Idle has descended at last to murder. While he chaffers with a receiver his female accomplice thrusts their victim's body through a trap-door in the floor, that it may be carried down to the secret-keeping river. But at this very moment she is betraying him for a price to the entering constables. In a remote corner of the room a normal Alsatian shindy, in which such weapons as chairs and fire-irons are in hearty use, is just at its height.

♣

Nor is Hogarth the only delineator of London low life who has immortalized Hanging Sword Alley. Here Dickens places the lodging of that honest tradesman (as he loved to think himself) Jerry Cruncher. Jerry, you remember, was the odd man outside Tellson's bank, in Fleet Street, who ran messages and piloted rich old ladies across the roadway. And a peculiar thing about Jerry was that he often left the bank in the evening with nice clean boots, yet woke up in Hanging Sword Alley next morning to find them so heavily clogged with clay that they became even better missiles than usual to throw at Mrs. Cruncher, when he saw her on her knees, praying against him and his business and his luck, as he obdurately believed. Life in Hanging Sword Alley was embittered for Mr. Cruncher by his wife's "flopping" propensities, and was only brightened when his hopeful boy asked him one day, apropos of his clay-clogged boots, " *Father, what's a Resurrection man ?* "

♣   ♣   ♣

ST. PAUL'S RAILINGS.

The great semi-circle of iron railings which formerly guarded the space in front of St. Paul's Cathedral was removed about fifty years ago. These railings dated from the reign of Queen Anne, and were said to have cost £12,000. In 1874, when the street was widened, they were sold for less than £350. Five of them may now be seen let into the wall at the foot of the lane leading round the Castle at Lewes. Their removal to this spot was appropriate because they had been made of the best old Sussex charcoal iron, a commodity long banished from the iron market. They were cast about the year 1710. The " State entrance gates " went with the railings, and were offered by Messrs. Davies, of Vauxhall, for " a lump sum of £150." All the English Sovereigns who had come to St. Paul's for fifty years had passed through these gates. The splendid old iron-work thus removed was nearly the last specimen of Sussex iron.

♣

Another small batch of the railings went to

Toronto, where, in the High Park, they still enclose the tomb of one John George Howard and his wife. On a brass plate is inscribed the verse :—

St. Paul's Cathedral for 160 years I did inclose,
   O stranger, look with reverence.
Man! man! unstable man!
   It was thou who caused the severance.

The preservation of these railings at Toronto is the more remarkable because the steamship *Delta*, which took them out, was wrecked, and they were recovered by salvage men.

♣   ♣   ♣

COCK-FIGHTING IN LONDON.

Several London street names are derived from the old sport of cock-fighting which, though illegal, is still practised in England. Cockspur Street, on the south side of Trafalgar Square, was named from the fighting-cocks' spurs which were sold in it for the use of the " fancy," who frequented the Whitehall and St. James's cockpits. To prove this origin is another thing; conjecture is the breath of such etymologies; but Mr. Holden Macmichael, our chief authority on the Charing Cross neighbourhood, favours the tradition, and states that within recent years cock-spurs have been purchasable in the street or its neighbourhood. The old White-hall cockpit was but a stone's throw from Cock-spur Street. Its history is a study in the evolution of respectability. First it was a cockpit pure and simple, then a theatre, then a congeries of State lodgings, and finally the Privy Council Office. Thus it befell that the arena of Henry VII's barbarous pleasures became the customary scene of George III's speech before the opening of Parliament.

♣

In his immensely interesting and curious " Book for a Rainy Day," John Thomas Smith says that in 1775 the following cockpits flourished in London, affording " high amusement to the unfeeling part of London's inhabitants ":—

1. The Royal Cockpit in the Birdcage Walk, St. James's Park. This Royal Cockpit afforded Hogarth characters for one of the worst of his subjects, though best of plates.

2. In Bainbridge Street, St. Giles's.

3. Near Gray's Inn Lane.

4. In Pickle-Egg Walk.

5. At the New Vauxhall Gardens, in St. George's-in-the-East.

6. That at the White Horse, Old Gravel Lane, near Hughes's late riding-school, at the foot of Blackfriars Bridge.

So early as 1709 Hatton, in his " New Year of London," says that the cockpit behind Gray's Inn enjoyed " the only vogue." Mr. William Boulton, in his " Amusements of Old London," quotes a description of this elegant resort by one Von Uffenbach, a German traveller.

Hogarth's print of the Royal Cockpit, referred to above, contains the whole gamut of cockpit passions. The main is presided over by Lord Albemarle Bertie, who enjoyed the sport none the less because, being blind, he could not see it. On the floor of the pit, where two cocks are inquiring each other's intentions with every nerve astretch, a curious shadow falls—the shadow of a defaulting backer who, for lack of a horse-pond, has been drawn up to the ceiling in a basket, whence he is dangling a watch which is apparently not regarded as legal tender.

When Charles Townley was filling his sculpture galleries at No. 7, Park Street, now Queen Anne's Gate, with the priceless relics of the arts of Greece and Rome, he found the cockpit next door a very noisy neighbour. Nor did he, by eleven years, live to see its removal. This was ordered in 1816, when it dawned on the authorities of Christ's Hospital, who owned the site, that to run a school for young gentlemen at one end of the town and a cockpit for old gentlemen at the other might savour of inconsistency. They declined to renew the lease. A new cockpit was immediately built in Tufton Street, Westminster, with the Royal arms, if you please, over the door. Here that versatile sportsman, Grantley Berkeley, saw his first main, and thither (he tells us) " the grandfather of the present Duke of Norfolk—attired in the sky-blue dress which, when I was a boy, I had often seen, with large ruffles at his wrists, with which, on shading, he would at times wipe out the pan of his gun—went to see one of the greatest ' mains' of the day."

♣ ♣ ♣

"CORNER MEMORY" THOMPSON.

In February, 1843, there died, at the age of eighty-six, this remarkable person, whose eccentric success had become matter of public interest. John Thompson was a native of St. Giles's, where his father was a greengrocer. As he advanced in life, he sought retirement, and on a spot just below Hampstead Church, built for himself, without plan or order,

M 2

"Frognal Priory," an assemblage of grotesque structures, but without any right of road to it, which he had to purchase at a great price.

❧

Thence, Thompson often went to town in his chariot, to collect curiosities for Frognal Priory, and these, for a time, he would show to any person who rang at his gate. He was designated "Corner Memory" from his having, for a bet, drawn a plan of St. Giles's parish from memory, at three sittings, specifying every coach-turning, stable-yard, and public pump, and likewise the *corner shop* of every street. He possessed a mechanical memory; for he could, by reading a newspaper overnight, repeat the whole of it next morning—an accomplishment more unusual than enviable.

❧   ❧   ❧

A HEAD FROM TOWER HILL.

In the " Vicar's cupboard " in the church of St. Botolph, Aldgate, is preserved a dread relic of an historic Tower Hill beheading. It is the head of Henry Grey, Duke of Suffolk, who was beheaded on Tower Hill, on February 23rd, 1554, eleven days after the execution of his illustrious daughter, Lady Jane Grey. Nearly sixty years ago, the head was found in a vault in a bed of oak sawdust, and its preservation is thought to have been the effect of the oak tannin.

♣

The presence of the head in the church is not inexplicable. Sir Thomas More's head was secured by Margaret Roper, and Sir Walter Raleigh's by Lady Raleigh. The Duke bore himself well on the scaffold, and was not perturbed when a man in front of the crowd called out at the last moment, " My lord, how shall I do for the money that you owe me? " Suffolk replied, " Alas, good fellow, I pray thee trouble me not now, but go thy way to my officers " He then paid his larger debt to the law.

♣   ♣   ♣

THE ROMANCE OF WATERLOO BRIDGE.

While its future existence is trembling in the balance of public necessity, every Londoner must be interested in Waterloo Bridge. It is a mistake to suppose, as some people do, that it was built to celebrate the victory of Waterloo. Its origin was much more prosaic. In the year 1809 a company was formed with a capital of £100,000 and sanction was sought from Parliament to build a temporary wooden bridge: the idea of the promoters being that a permanent stone bridge could be built later out of the large profits to be obtained from the tolls on persons and vehicles passing over. The City of London opposed the plan for three successive sessions in Parliament; and the company was finally compelled to abandon the project of a wooden bridge and undertake the construction of a stone one. In order to do this they increased their capital by an additional £400,000, but so assured were they of the remuneration to be derived from the toll that this large sum was immediately raised among themselves, and the shares were at a guinea premium the next day.

♣

The first plan of the bridge was prepared by George Dodds, a well-known engineer of the day, but the managing committee were not satisfied with his design, and referred it to John Rennie and a Mr. Jessop for their opinion. These gentlemen reported that for the most part it was a copy of M. Peyronnet's celebrated bridge at Neuilly, with modifications rendered necessary by the difference of situation, and the greater width of the river to be spanned. They also pointed out several objections to Dodds's design, as well as to the plan he proposed for founding the piers, and as a result of their report this plan was abandoned. When an Act was passed in 1809 authorizing the " Strand Bridge Company " to build a stone bridge from " some part of the precinct of the Savoy, to the opposite shore at Cupar's Bridge in Lambeth," the committee again applied to Rennie, and requested him to furnish a design.

John Rennie was then rising to the front rank in his profession. He prepared two designs for what was then called the Strand Bridge, one of seven equal arches and the other of nine; the second being eventually chosen by the committee as the less costly. The first stone was laid on October 11th, 1811, by Mr. H. Swan, M.P., when a block of Cornish granite was lowered over an excavation containing gold and silver coins of the realm. A story of the construction of the bridge worth recording is given here practically as it occurs in Dr. Smiles's " Lives of the Engineers." Most of the stone required during the construction of the bridge was hewn in some fields on the Surrey side. It was brought thence upon trucks drawn along railways, in the first instance over temporary bridges of wood; and it is a remarkable circumstance that nearly the whole of the material was drawn by one horse, known as " Old Jack "— a most sensible animal and a great favourite. His driver was, generally speaking, a steady and trustworthy man, though he had a weakness for a dram before breakfast. As the railway along which the trucks were drawn passed in front of a public-house door, the horse and truck were usually pulled up while Tom entered for his morning aid. On one occasion the driver stayed so long that " Old Jack," becoming impatient, poked his head into the open door, and taking his master's coat-collar between his teeth (Smiles tells us this was done in a " gentle sort of manner "), pulled him out from the midst of his companions and thus forced him to carry on.

As the work neared completion, its name was changed from " Strand " to " Waterloo " Bridge in memory of the great battle of June 18th, 1815, and although it could have been opened earlier than it was the great day was postponed until the anniversary of the battle, June 18th, 1817. The scene was a magnificent one, and congratulations rained upon the architect. John Constable was a spectator, and his commemorative picture was exhibited at the Royal Academy, Writing to a friend after the ceremony, Rennie remarked: " I had a hard business to escape knighthood at the opening." Rennie, in fact, preferred to be known to fame as plain John Rennie, the architect of Waterloo Bridge, which the great Canova pronounced to be " a colossal monument worthy of Sesostris and the Cæsars."

♣   ♣   ♣

"THAT PLEASANT PLACE."

Thou art in London—in that pleasant place
Where every kind of mischief's daily brew-
ing.   BYRON.—" Don Juan."

♣   ♣   ♣

THE HONEST SOLICITOR.

In St. Dunstan's Church, Fleet Street, the following unique epitaph may be seen:—

To the memory of
Hobson Judkin, Esq.,
Late of Clifford's Inn,
THE HONEST SOLICITOR,
who departed this life June the 30, 1812.
This tablet was erected by his Clients as a token
of Gratitude and Respect for his honest, faithful,
and friendly Conduct to them thro' Life.
Go, Reader, and imitate
Hobson Judkin.

Alexander Pope declared that an honest man's the noblest work of God; are we, then, to say that an honest solicitor is the noblest product of the Law? Each statement wears the double face of truth and cynicism. It is enough to be honest, like Hobson Judkin.

♣   ♣   ♣

THE PEDLAR AND HIS DOG.

The great home of the London County Council, at the east end of Westminster Bridge, occupies the site of a field long known as Pedlar's Acre. The tradition is that a prosperous pedlar had a favourite dog which, when it died, he wanted to bury in the churchyard of St. Mary's, Lambeth, close to Lambeth Palace, and that he gave this ground to the parish in return for the favour. The story may be an invention, but for more than three centuries a window in an aisle of St. Mary's church has contained a representation of a pedlar and his dog.

♣   ♣   ♣

AN EMBLEM OF ETERNITY.

Charles Lamb, on the top of Skiddaw, thought about the ham-and-beef shop in St. Martin's Lane. That ham-and-beef shop must have been rather famous in its day, for it is surely the same establishment mentioned in a story of Henry Fuseli, the eccentric Italian who became one of our early Royal Academicians. Fuseli told a sculptor that the familiar emblem of eternity, a serpent with its tail in its mouth, which he had carved on a monument would not do at all. "It won't do, I tell you; you must have something new." The sculptor asked how he could find anything new for the purpose. "Oh, nothing so easy," said Fuseli. "I'll help you to it. When I went away to Rome, I left two fat men cutting fat bacon in St. Martin's Lane; in ten years' time I returned, and found the two fat men cutting fat bacon still; twenty more years have passed, and there the two fat fellows cut the fat flitches the same as ever. Carve them—if they look not like an image of eternity I know not what does."

♣   ♣   ♣

Go where we may, rest where we will,
Eternal London haunts us still.

Thomas Moore.

Murray's Modern London 1860

Although essentially a guide for visitors, this book is also an excellent read containing well written descriptions of pretty well everything a tourist might wish to know if he were visiting London a century and a half ago.

Packed with well researched facts and statistics we can wander around the streets, markets and fine buildings being told who lived where, what treasures may be found within, the volume of trade conducted in the markets, the number of patients in the hospitals and the courses available at universities and colleges. We also visit prisons, exhibitions, clubs and societies, residences of the famous, sites associated with remarkable events and witness the diverse commodities passing through the docks.

Much can also be learned about how daily life then differed from today. Some things were better such as the workings of the Post Office 'letters posted before 6 in the evening would be delivered the same evening within 3 miles'. But much was worse such as the appalling sewage arrangements. 'The daily discharge into the Thames would cover 36 acres to a depth of 6 feet' but already there was an understanding of pollution and sewage works were planned.

A jewel of a book for anyone wishing to explore London during the first half of Victoria's reign.

Enquire Within upon everything - 1890

In the wake of the Industrial Revolution the population swiftly developed a thirst for knowledge about the myriad of new goods and ideas that were becoming available. But before the days of television, newspaper advertising and junk mail how did people get to know about everything? Over a million people solved the problem by buying a copy of this book which caused a publishing sensation in Victorian Britain. Because it explained so much about so many different aspects of life it continues to provide a very enjoyable and comprehensive peep into the lifestyle of our forebears.

Old House Books, Moretonhampstead, Devon, TQ13 8PA. UK
www.OldHouseBooks.co.uk   info@OldHouseBooks.co.uk   01647 440707

Other Victorian and Edwardian facsimile reprints from Old House Books

Baedeker's London and its Environs 1900

This comprehensive guide takes us on a tour of the world's greatest city at the close of the Victorian era.

All major sites are described in detail. There are 33 walking tours including The City, St. Paul's, Regent's Park Zoo and London Docks and a dozen by river steamer and train including The Crystal Palace, Windsor Castle and as far afield as Rochester and St.Albans. Each is packed with directions, historical facts, travel arrangements and prices.

The advice on etiquette, security, accommodation, travel to and within Britain and recommended shops paint a fascinating picture of life a century ago. There is a history of London.

Over 500 pages, a fold out map, plans of notable buildings and 31 pages of coloured street plans, printed facsimile from the original edition. A source of fascination for anyone wishing to explore London a century ago.

The British Empire world map 1905

As the twentieth century dawned the British Empire enjoyed its heyday. This map shows British possessions coloured red at a time when it spanned eleven and a half million square miles with 400 million inhabitants.

This colour reproduction of a contemporary world map shows details of global trade, including: the furs of fox, bear, seal and otter brought from the shores of Canada's Lake Athabasca by canoes in summer and dog sleds in winter; cochineal, indigo and vanilla from central America; teak and bamboo from Siam; cinnamon and pearls from Ceylon; tortoise shells and birds of paradise from New Guinea as well as minerals and foodstuffs from all over the world. In the Sahara we note that slaves were still being traded. Four other maps show the development of the empire in the previous four hundred years.

Coaling stations, telegraph cables, railways and caravan routes are all marked. A ten-page gazetteer describes over 200 British countries and possessions as well as 33 (including Normandy and the USA) which had been lost to the crown.

Old House Books, Moretonhampstead, Devon, TQ13 8PA. UK
www.OldHouseBooks.co.uk   info@OldHouseBooks.co.uk   01647 440707

Other Victorian and Edwardian facsimile reprints from
Old House Books

A Street Map of London, 1843

One of the earliest detailed street maps of London published over a century and a half ago so that passengers in Hansom cabs could check that they were being taken by the shortest route.

Faithfully reproducing the original hand colouring, it shows street names, prominent buildings, docks, factories, canals and the earliest railways in minute detail.

Beyond the limits of the developed area, which in 1843 extended no further than Hyde Park in the west and Stepney in the east, can be seen the orchards and market gardens of Chelsea and Southwark, the marshes of the Isle of Dogs and the outlying villages of Earls Court, Kentish Town and Bow.

Each map is accompanied by a history of London in 1843 which helps to set the scene as you embark on your journey through the greatest city in the world early in the reign of Queen Victoria.

Compare this map to Bacon's Map of London 1902 to see the massive development that took place during the Victorian era.

Bacon's Up to date map of London, 1902

The reign of no other monarch saw such extensive changes as those which took place when Queen Victoria was on the throne. This street map of London originally published at the end of her long life provides a perfect contrast with the map of London 1843. Gone are the orchards of Chelsea and the marshes of The Isle of Dogs. Earl's Court and other villages lying beyond the built up area at the beginning of her reign have now been swallowed by the expanding conurbation.

There is massive development and activity on the lower reaches of the Thames where there is much evidence of the new docks servicing the needs of both the Empire and the mother country.

Many of the underground railway lines we know today have already been built. But there was much more to be completed during the coming century and places such as Willesden and Herne Hill were still surrounded by countryside in 1902.

Old House Books, Moretonhampstead, Devon, TQ13 8PA. UK
www.OldHouseBooks.co.uk   info@OldHouseBooks.co.uk   01647 440707

Other Victorian and Edwardian facsimile reprints from Old House Books

Dickens's Dictionary of London, 1888

An unconventional Victorian guidebook which vividly captures the atmosphere and vitality of what was then the largest city in the world, the heart, not just of the nation, but also of a great empire. Through a series of over 700 detailed entries contained in 272 pages printed facsimile from the original 1888 edition, we build up a living portrait of Victorian London, from the fashionable gentlemen's clubs of St James's to the markets and slums of the East End. 1888 was the year of the Jack The Ripper murders. The remarks on the principal buildings, the churches and the great railway stations, the banks, theatres and sporting facilities are informative and well observed, the comments of someone who obviously knew London like the back of his hand.

Equally revealing and very entertaining are the wealth of tips on social behaviour. There is essential advice on everything from the hiring of servants (a parlour maid's recommended salary was £12 per annum), the benefits of cycling (most welcome in view of the saving of cruelty to horseflesh), how to cope with milk contaminated with diphtheria and typhoid, fogs (much appreciated by the predatory classes) through to avoiding the attention of carriage thieves.

Dickens's Dictionary of The Thames, 1887

A fascinating portrait of the river at the height of its Victorian prosperity. On the upper Thames it was the carefree era of regattas and riverside picnics, while London's tideway and great docks were busy with the comings and goings of barges, steamers and sailing ships servicing the world's largest port and the Empire on which the sun never set.

This treasure trove of a book has descriptions of the villages and towns along the river from its source near Cricklade to the Nore Lightship. It is packed with practical advice, maps of popular destinations, locations of angling and bathing spots. Riverside inns to accommodate oarsmen are listed with details of how to return boats by train at a time when an annual season ticket between Windsor and Paddington cost as little as £18.

Old House Books, Moretonhampstead, Devon, TQ13 8PA. UK
www.OldHouseBooks.co.uk info@OldHouseBooks.co.uk 01647 440707

Other Victorian and Edwardian facsimile reprints from Old House Books

Oarsman's & Angler's Thames map, 1893

Explore Britain's best loved waterway with the map that must surely have been used by the *Three Men in a Boat*. Very detailed, one inch to the mile and over 8 feet in length, it shows all 164 miles from the source to London Bridge. Riverside towns and villages are marked with historical information and details of the locks and how to operate them.

For fishermen, the best pools where trout, pike, perch and others were to be found. There are also details of toll charges and angling laws and a description of life on the river over a century ago when the Thames was the nation's favourite place for recreation and sport with as many as 30,000 anglers and 12,000 small boats regularly using the river. The Great Western and Southern Railways delivered hordes of Londoners to the area for steamer trips, regattas and riverside picnics.

The English Companion

In this witty and stylish companion to Englishness Sunday Times columnist Godfrey Smith takes us on a leisurely but perceptive tour of all that he holds dear in England and the English. It is very much an informal ramble, as if in the company of an old friend. He treats us to a display of sparkling and knowledgeable comments on our national life from Churchill to Pubs, Elgar to Rugby, Bertie Wooster to George Orwell, British Beef to the National Lottery and from Fish and Chips to Evelyn Waugh.

'A most entertaining book' Kingsley Amis

'A mixture of eccentricity & scholarship, highly entertaining' A.J.P.Taylor

Old House Books, Moretonhampstead, Devon, TQ13 8PA. UK
www.OldHouseBooks.co.uk info@OldHouseBooks.co.uk 01647 440707